Book Description

How many times have you created goals that you never seemed to achieve? Maybe you told yourself you were going to quit spending money frivolously but felt tempted to buy an item online? If you can identify yourself as someone who can't seem to follow through with their intentions, this book is for you!

Have you ever wondered why it's so hard to stick with your plans or honor your own words? You may have told yourself that this year you are determined to lose weight, but struggle to stay committed to your fitness program. Relax. You are not weird! In fact, there are so many people just like you who have not discovered the secret to permanent life transformation.

Do you want to know what the secret is? Okay, here it goes: If you want to change your life for good, you need to master your habits.

Experiencing positive change in your life goes beyond self-control. Your brain is always learning and categorizing information even when you are not aware of it. It doesn't separate good information from bad information; it only records and stores. Take a moment and think about the kind of information you might have stored in your brain right now. Is it information that can assist you in making positive life changes or will it hinder you?

As soon as your brain forms a habit, you are at the mercy of your habit until you decide to reprogram how you think about yourself and your life. The good news is once you learn how habits develop and how to replace bad ones with good ones, you will have more control over which direction your life takes!

In this book, author Ahmad Jamal Alassadi will offer you the ultimate breakdown of the power behind habit formation and how you can purposefully create habits which help you achieve your goals, cultivate happiness and live a life rich with meaning. After reading this book, you will feel empowered to take back control over your mind and break free from negative patterns of behavior and thought.

Mastering Your Habits

A Practical Guide To Creating Good Habits, Success, and Happiness

Ahmad Jamal Alassadi

advice. The content within this book has been derived from various sources. Please consult a licensed professional before attempting any techniques outlined in this book.

By reading this document, the reader agrees that under no circumstances is the author responsible for any losses, direct or indirect, that are incurred as a result of the use of the information contained within this document, including, but not limited to, errors, omissions, or inaccuracies.

Table of Contents

Introduction

Roy T. Bennet once said, "Attitude is a choice. Happiness is a choice. Optimism is a choice. Kindness is a choice. Giving is a choice. Respect is a choice. Whatever choice you make makes you. Choose wisely " Someone may look at this quote and say, "I choose happiness, however, happiness doesn't choose me." In other words, as much as they desire happiness, their life is marked with obstacles and inner conflict.

What do we do in such cases? How do we align our external reality with our internal reality? How can we successfully cultivate the kind of emotional state or mindset that we desire? If you have ever reflected on these questions you'll understand how frustrating it is to want something so badly but struggle to achieve it. Even when you've told yourself that you are putting in 100% effort, there still seems to be a barrier keeping you from realizing your goals.

Many people end up feeling cursed when life does not go according to their plans. They believe God is against them and every circumstance is working to keep them down. Is there any truth to this? Could they really be cursed and is God angry with them? Assuming that it isn't true, what answer can we give to these people to motivate them to continue seeking their dreams?

I would answer them in three words: Change your mind. The definition of insanity is doing the same thing over and over again and expecting the same results. If you live your life in only one way and so far have achieved only one result, it is time to change how you do things. The intention of this book is to help people who are seeking to make positive change in their lives learn how to change their minds.

It's More Than What You See

True change must start at the root. When you want to remove weeds in your garden, you must pull them from the root, otherwise the plants will grow back in a matter of days. Likewise, when you seek permanent life transformation, you must establish a new order of thinking. Your thoughts are the roots of everything you see with your naked eye. Take a look around you and notice how many different things you see. The technological devices, design, and engineering of every object you are surrounded by were all conceived in the minds of great people men and women. They began as ideas or concepts which were nurtured until they became physical manifestations.

Just as innovators create physical products or technology from ideas, your mind has the power to create and shape your reality based on your thoughts. To test this phenomenon, I would like you to be my test subject in a quick experiment: Relax your body and close your eyes. Think for a moment about a happy memory from your childhood. What happened? How did it make you feel? As you think about this memory, I would like you to notice the sensations going through your body. Are you more excitable? Do you feel a sense of warmth? Open your eyes. This simple experiment explores the power of your thoughts. By recalling a memory, you can change your physiology and improve your mood.

In this particular experiment, we focused on a positive thought. However, negative thoughts operate in a similar manner. The more time you spend dwelling on a negative thought, the greater the negative impact it has on your physiology, behaviors, and mental state. If the secret to permanent life transformation is to change your mind, then I suggest you learn how to control your thoughts, choosing only the best! Failure to control your thoughts may lead to behaviors that are toxic, self-destructive, and unhealthy.

Mastering Your Habits

Show me your habits and I will show you your future. Habits are neither good nor bad. They are the brain's way of automating certain tasks so that it can reduce the amount of information it has to process. Imagine how unproductive you would be if you had to consciously think of every task you did throughout the day. Not only would you be unproductive, but you would end up stressed and fatigued as well. The brain picks up on patterns of behavior and over time learns these patterns so that it can cue the body to perform them subconsciously.

The danger however, comes when some of these patterns are negative thoughts, behaviors, and beliefs. The brain cannot separate a negative thought from a positive one, and neither does it have the time to do so. When you develop negative habits, it means one thing: you have been dwelling on negativity for so long that your brain has picked up a negative pattern. This negative pattern becomes behavior that you perform even when you are not aware. For example, using curse words in your speech is harmless if you plan on doing it once or twice. However, when cursing becomes a way in which you express yourself, your brain picks it up as a pattern and soon enough, you are cursing subconsciously.

Many people look at their negative behaviors or self-limiting beliefs and wonder why they have such a discouraging perspective on life. They wonder where their insecurities started or why they find it so difficult to control themselves. The truth is most of what manifests in the physical had to begin with powerful thoughts (the root). These thoughts, regardless of whether they were positive or negative, were repeated long enough to become habitual. When a negative thought becomes a habit, it is difficult to break. How can you break a cycle you are not aware of 100% of the time?

Breaking bad habits and adopting positive habits is only possible when you address the root problem, which are your thoughts. In this book, I will teach you the secrets of how to make your habits work for you so your external reality can match the desires of your heart. The book will cover various aspects of creating new and positive habits so that you can prosper physically, mentally, emotionally, and spiritually. After reading this book, you will be empowered to prioritize your goals and fearlessly pursue them. I hope to leave you inspired to reclaim control over your life and truly believe that nothing is impossible for you!

Mastering your habits requires change and that change starts NOW.

Part 1: Good Habits

Have you ever wondered what a "good habit" looks or feels like? What characteristics make a habit "good?" I've spent many years studying habits and what distinguishes a good habit from a bad one. What I have found is that good habits are inherently positive. They have the power to charge your body with positive sensations and emotions. A good habit, like physical exercise, has the power to make you feel good about yourself afterward.

Since good habits are inherently positive, they also have the ability to positively influence other people. Let's face it, when a person is radiating from within, their energy is infectious. We want to be around them and adopt some of their habits so that we can also radiate with the same light. Good habits inspire those around us to invest in their own lives and tap into their own glory. Isn't this a wonderful thing?

Just as much as good habits can positively influence other people, they can also boost your self-confidence and improve your level of self-awareness. The next time you give a generous donation or practice gratitude, notice the rewarding feeling you have inside. Your acts of goodness can make you feel valuable, loved, and appreciated. When good habits become part of your life , you develop a love for goodness, peace, and everything righteous that can support your positive lifestyle.

For example, if you were a person who gossiped about other people, you may outgrow this behavior or become intolerant of it when you cultivate a lifestyle of good habits. Outgrowing bad habits and drawing closer to good habits will refine your character and mature you in ways you may have never expected. Overall, you become a better person and make a more significant contribution in the lives of others.

Part one of this book looks at various aspects of building good habits and incorporating them into your lifestyle. Some topics include how to manage your time and use it wisely, making your health your number one priority, and setting meaningful goals to guide you toward your desired future.

Chapter 1: Time! Let's Make the Best Use of It

How often do you reflect on the time you have in this lifetime? It is easy to think you have an abundance of time at your disposal and get carried away by meaningless pursuits. The truth is your time is finite. Just as you were born on a certain date, at a certain time, you will also leave this earth on a certain date, at a certain time. I don't say this to scare you, but rather to gently remind you to make better use of your time.

Take a moment and think about your daily tasks. If you have a daily planner, this would be a good time to take it out. Go through each task you perform on a daily basis and ask yourself why you do it. Why do you wake up in the morning? Why do you brush your teeth? Why do you drive to work? And so forth. Some of the answers to these questions will seem obvious. You brush your teeth because you don't want to offend anyone with smelly breath. However, you will see there are some tasks you don't have an explanation for.

One major time waster is using social media. Do you know how much time you spend flicking through photos of people you don't know? How else could you be using that time wisely? The reason social media is so addictive is because it provides an escape. You get lost in the multitude of videos and photos and forget about where you are or what you need to do for the rest of the day. Some people may see the escape offered by social media as a way to avoid or run away from present day troubles. For example, you may log onto social media at work to delay performing your work responsibilities or you may use social media to avoid social interactions.

Determining how you spend your time and making a conscious effort to use all 24 hours in a day wisely can help you succeed in life. It can help you prioritize your most important task while leaving enough room for you to reflect and recharge. When you learn how to make the best use of your time, you will never feel robbed of time at the end of the day. Instead, you will sleep peacefully without regrets about what you could have done with your time.

Live Intentionally

I love to ask people to explain the thought processes behind their choices. Sometimes a person can articulate the reason behind their decisions with a great amount of clarity. This shows me that the individual has thoroughly understood the cause and effect of their choices. There are also times when people look at me blankly when I ask. They are caught off guard by my question, as though they didn't understand why they were making the choice in the first place.

What happens when you don't fully understand why you have taken certain measures? The short answer is you have no control over the outcome. A good example to illustrate this would be applying for a job role you have no knowledge about. You may be desperate to find a job so you can contribute to the welfare of your family and subsequently apply to any available job vacancies. You don't understand some of the positions you are applying for but you don't really care; all you want is the security of a paycheck at the end of the month.

Assuming you get the job and the recruiter tells you to start immediately, how do you think your first day at work would go? Chaotic, to say the least. You would be asking colleagues many questions about how to operate the system and how to create quarterly reports and team presentations. Indeed, at the end of the month you would get your salary, however, the amount of stress and anxiety you would have to stomach wouldn't make the salary worth it.

The only way to avoid regretting your decisions is to live intentionally. Simply put, intentional living is about doing things with a sense of purpose. You recognize there are only a number of tasks you can perform in a day, and ensure everyone of them adds value to your life. Intentional living emphasizes the need to make good choices, since every choice can either add value or steal value from your life. Brushing your teeth is a good choice because it can improve your physical hygiene. Smoking, on the other hand, is a bad choice because with every puff, you compromise your physical well-being.

There are many people who will be offended by the concept of intentional living because it forces them to confront their bad choices. It also makes each person responsible and accountable for their own lives. When you decide to live intentionally, you cannot blame your environment for the actions or behaviors you take or don't take. You realize how much control you have over your emotions, thus making it easier to embrace emotions that add value to your life and releasing emotions that steal value from your life.

Living intentionally takes you off autopilot and back in the driver's seat of your life. You become more aware of the consequences each decision brings and feel a greater sense of urgency to make decisions which enhance your well-being. For example, you might reflect on your day and find you spent four hours sitting on the couch. You realize those four hours on the couch did not add any value to your life. This realization causes you to find more productive activities or projects to do during that four hour slot. If you have particular goals, you may use the four hours to do research or planning related to your goals. The four hour slot becomes a valuable part of your day that you use to prepare for your future ambitions.

5 Ways To Be More Intentional Throughout the Day

The good news about being more intentional with how you use your time is that it doesn't take long before you start seeing positive changes in your daily routine. Moreover, one intentional choice can inspire a series of intentional choices, adding more value to each day. I guarantee when you become aware of how you use your time, each day will look different and feel like a blessing. Below are five ways to be more intentional with your choices throughout the day:

1. Watch Your Media Consumption

Are you aware of the amount of media you consume on a daily basis? If not, I would suggest being mindful of each time you log onto your social media account, respond to Whatsapp messages, read online news articles, watch YouTube videos, or binge on Netflix. Engaging with your friends and family online or watching TV is not necessarily a bad choice when it is done intentionally. Intentional media consumption always has a bigger purpose. For example, you access social media to get a quick update on current affairs or you watch YouTube videos which are related to a project you are working on. When media is consumed with purpose it can become an extremely valuable part of your day.

2. Choose Kindness

When you make a conscious decision to show others kindness, you are choosing who you want to be and what you want to stand for in each moment. Intentionality doesn't only relate to what we do, but also to who we are. Even though you cannot control how other people behave, you have full control over your own behaviors and how you leave others feeling. Choose kindness, not because you are waiting for kindness in return, but because you have chosen to be a kind human being.

3. Find Activities That Bring You Joy

We cannot separate value from intentional living. When you are intentional about your choices, you add value to your day. This in turn brings you a lot of joy. Interchangeably, when you focus on activities which bring you a lot of joy, your activities become valuable parts of your day and thus echo the principles of intentional living. If you don't enjoy your current job, find an activity after work that brings joy into your heart. It can be painting, cooking, or spending quality time with loved ones. This will ensure you always feel rewarded by at least one activity every day.

4. Challenge Your Purchasing Decisions

Mindless consumption has never made anyone happy; all it does is burn a hole through your wallet. Whenever you feel tempted to spend money on a product or service, ask yourself what value the product or service holds. Will it help you perform your daily tasks efficiently? Will you be able to improve upon the quality of your work? It's not enough to purchase a product or service because "it feels good". There are so many things that have the power to make you feel good which are absolutely free. If you cannot provide a good justification for why you need to make the purchase, it is best to leave it alone and find other positive self-care practices to make you feel good about yourself.

5. Listen Without Waiting To Respond

It is important to learn how to listen intentionally, without waiting to make an argument. Active listening requires you to focus on what the other person is saying so that you can understand their experience. Active listening saves you time because once you have heard the message, you can respond immediately and avoid misunderstandings. Great places to practice active listening is at work, when taking instructions, or when engaging in dialogue with others.

Honor Your Word, Honor Your Time

I once had a friend I loved dearly, although one thing irritated me about him: he never honored his word. We would make a plan to meet for lunch and my friend would call me 30 minutes before our scheduled meetings to tell me he couldn't make it, or to reschedule for a later time. After repeating the same behavior a few more times, I decided to confront him about how disrespectful and inconsiderate his actions were and how it made me not desire to see him. He listened to my frustrations and told me his bad behavior was affecting other parts of his life, as well. For example, he would agree to submit a work report by a certain deadline and when the time came, the report wouldn't be complete. He asked me to help him find ways of being accountable to his words and actions, because he feared one day his bad behavior would bring devastating consequences.

When you develop a habit of not honoring your word, you compromise the quality of your relationships and waste a significant amount of time in the process. Your friends, colleagues, or business associates may turn the other direction when they see you coming. By not holding yourself accountable for promises you've made, you have undermined your own integrity. No one trusts that you will do what you say you will do and thus, no one feels comfortable depending on you.

The failure to honor your word is also a type of self-sabotage. You are unable to follow through with the goals you have set, or meet work targets that can improve your chances of landing a promotion. Whenever you are given opportunities to take on responsibility, you may feel ill-prepared, unworthy, or unqualified for the opportunity. This may cause you to procrastinate getting the task done, ultimately jeopardizing any prospect receiving the same opportunity again.

When you fail to honor your words, you waste a lot of your own time. Rescheduling plans or leaving things for tomorrow creates unnecessary delays, which eat up valuable time. If you told yourself you are determined to go back to school and finish your degree this year but failed to honor your word, you would have to push back your plan for another year. This may seem insignificant, but since you have a finite number of days to live out your dreams, wasting a year is a big deal!

It's important to learn to honor your word so you can feel satisfied with your life. You deserve to live the kind of lifestyle where you can see how much progress you have made by simply following your plans and actively pursuing your goals. Wouldn't it feel good to wake up in an apartment you have always dreamed of living in? Or feel a sense of fulfillment in your relationships? Below are a few tips you can start practicing to help you stay accountable to your word:

Tip 1: Avoid Overselling What You Can Do

When you interact with other people, you naturally want to present yourself in the best light. This is especially true when you are meeting new people you want to impress. While it is good to present your strengths, it is important not to oversell yourself and risk being perceived as someone you are not. Overselling what you can do for others can put you in a position where you are unable to deliver on your promises. This would lead to you feeling pressured to perform at a level you are unfamiliar or uncomfortable with. Thus, when expressing who you are, remember to paint an authentic picture so that others can appreciate the real you.

Tip 2: Keep a Diary or Planner

You might have a good memory, but all of us are guilty of forgetting our mental notes. Keeping a diary or daily planner will help you structure your tasks each day and schedule additional tasks when you are available. A planner will also ensure you don't have any overlapping tasks and, if you wish, you can add 15 to 30 minute breaks in between tasks to give you a moment to yourself.

Tip 3: Avoid Making Empty Promises

When you know you cannot attend an event or fulfill someone's request, it is better to be honest and politely decline the invitation or say you are too busy to assist them. I find that people respond well to straightforward communication because it leaves no room for any misunderstandings. There will be times where you need to tell someone whether you can or cannot commit to a plan. Make sure you follow through and message them with your decision, instead of keeping quiet and assuming your silence speaks louder than your words.

Tip 4: Ask for Help

Many times, people overcommit themselves to plans because they are afraid to ask for help. They figure asking for help may come across as a sign of their inadequacy in fulfilling the tasks at hand. This is not true. Asking for help shows commitment to completing your tasks to the best of your ability. It shows that you care so much about your tasks that you don't want to compromise the results by spreading yourself too thin. There are many people around you, whether in your personal or professional life, who are willing to carry some of the burdens on your shoulders when you feel overwhelmed.

Put First Things First

What does it mean to put first things first? It is very simple: It is to decide what deserves your attention in each moment and forget about everything else. For example, in the mornings while preparing to go to work, prioritize your quiet time. In that moment, nothing else matters besides listening to your thoughts and checking in with your emotions. At work, prioritize all of your work tasks, including work meetings and work calls. If you happened to receive a call from your cousin, ignore it because it isn't a matter of priority at work. After work, you can use this time to return your cousin's phone call since your focus would be on spending quality time with your family.

There are going to be many people or tasks each day that are going to fight for your attention. Your spouse may urge you to fix something around the house, your children might demand time to discuss a holiday trip, and your boss at work could command focus away from a task you're doing. It is unfortunate that you cannot split yourself among these people or be at two places at the same time. Thus, part of making progress each day requires you to organize your priorities and proceed with the tasks that matter most to you.

Setting intentions for your day benefits you by giving each day a sense of purpose. It helps you take direction in your life.. Intentions create order in your day to avoid becoming overwhelmed. In other words, you achieve a greater amount of stability and can easily prioritize and complete important tasks.

Prioritizing important tasks will structure your life, put you in charge of your time, and give you control of your environment. Instead of attempting to process large amounts of information at one time, you only focus on processing information that matters NOW. The world will have you believe that everything matters, all of the time, but this isn't true. There are times where your well-being is a priority and other times where the well-being of your loved ones is a priority. Knowing how to create this structure will propel you to succeed. Below are three simple steps on how to organize your life and create clear priorities:

Step 1: Create Clear Boundaries

You need to know when and how to draw the line with others. Depending on your life, you may be juggling a lot of roles. You may be a parent, spouse, sibling, child, colleague, boss, friend, or mentor. If you attempted to perform all of these roles at once, you'd faint from exhaustion! It's difficult enough being a parent *and* a spouse in addition to all the other roles you are expected to fill.

Setting clear boundaries helps you gently decline an invitation or request when you are busy with other tasks. By declining the invitation or request, you are not saying you don't want to help, but rather you are too preoccupied at that moment to be of any assistance. If your children were to run into the office during the busiest time of your work day, asking you to help them with an urgent matter, what would your response be? As much as you love your children and desire to support them in as many ways as you can, their urgent request would be inappropriate. Since you are at work and your mind is focused on being as productive as you can, you can only address requests that are work-related. After hours, or during weekends, your children have much more of your time since the role of mother or father takes up a good portion of your life.

Setting clear boundaries, especially with loved ones, can be very difficult. For some reason, we tend to struggle saying "No" to the people closest to us. However, if saying "No" can help you put first things first, then it may be the best thing for you to do. The word "No" sounds like rejection, but it doesn't have to be. Saying "No" simply means you are choosing to say "Yes" to something else. For example, if you say "No" to going out with your friends, you are saying "Yes" to staying indoors and recharging after a long day. Likewise, if you say "No" to answering emails in the evenings, you are saying "Yes" to dedicating your evenings to yourself or to your family. In essence, by declining one request, you are approving another one. Adopting this perspective makes it easier for you to boldly say "No" without feeling guilty for accepting someone's requests.

Step 2: Create Clear Objectives

Step two is all about creating a plan to help you maintain your priorities and avoid going off track. For example, if you intend on giving your full attention to your job while at work, you need to have a plan detailing how you would maximize your time and put it to good use. The best way to do this is to create clear objectives. Objectives tell you what you can expect or what you can work toward when achieving your goals. Even though your mind is willing to adopt new behaviors, you need to feed your mind new expectations.

Objectives are small tasks that make a huge impact when strung together. These tasks don't have to be complicated at all; the most effective objectives are those you can perform easily without burdening yourself. Take a moment and think about a typical day in your life. Divide your day into three parts. You can decide how you want to divide your day depending on your current lifestyle. If you are a working professional, you can divide your day into before work, at work, and after work. If you are a stay-at-home mother, you can divide your day into the morning rush, quiet time alone, and after children come back home. For each part of your day, you will set clear objectives to help you set priorities specific to that period. Remember to keep your objectives realistic and actionable so that you can easily perform them.

Below is an example of how a university student would set clear objectives for their day:

Before school

- 10 minutes of quiet time (prayer, meditation, reflection, etc.)
- Shower and get dressed.
- Eat a nutrient-rich meal.
- Pack school lunch.
- Look at my daily planner and reflect on the day's tasks.

At school

- Take down notes in lectures.
- Visit the library to drop off and pick up books.
- Spend 30 minutes in the computer labs researching school-related information.
- Spend 30 minutes eating lunch with my friends.

After school

- Take a 45 minute nap.
- Prepare an afternoon snack to eat.
- Complete homework assignments.
- Prepare and eat dinner.
- Watch an episode of my favorite show.
- Brush my teeth and prepare for bed.
- 10 minutes of quiet time (prayer, meditation, reflection, etc.)

By dividing their daily tasks into three categories, it would help the student prioritize specific tasks at specific times during the day. At the end of the day, they would be proud of how much they have accomplished, by simply organizing their daily tasks better.

Step 3: Practice!

Once you have set clear boundaries and created clear objectives, all that's left for you to do is practice your new routine until it becomes a way of life. Trust me, one day or one week of practicing setting boundaries won't make it stick in your mind. You need to be consistent in saying "No" and compartmentalizing every task you need to complete by the end of the day. There will be times where you are tempted to cross over your own boundaries. Be patient with yourself in these moments and remind yourself how gratifying it is to have a sense of structure in your life. Your boundaries are not built to hurt you or limit your freedom; they are actually put in place to protect your freedom and give you an opportunity to spend your time according to your own desires.

You may also find your friends or family members resisting this new structure you are building. Take time to express the benefits of this new structure in your life and how it brings a sense of peace in everything you do. Reassure your loved ones that you value them and have designated a special slot to completely focus on strengthening your relationships with them.

Chapter 2: Goal Setting Motivating Yourself To Turn Your Visions Into Reality

If you ask anybody what their five or ten year goals are, they will go on a 10 minute ramble detailing the career, health, and personal success they envision for themselves. Follow up by asking them what they have done to start actioning some of these goals, however, and you will hear excuses or a simple "Nothing". Over the years, I have found that many people don't struggle with expressing their dreams and future ambitions, although they do struggle with taking the necessary steps to manifest them.

There are so many factors affecting a person's motivation or desire to pursue their goals. Many people wait for external conditions to be favorable before they can start. They believe in pursuing their goals when life circumstances look and feel perfect. For example, someone might say "I will only start exercising when I can afford a gym membership." This person is under the impression that they can only pursue their fitness goal once their financial situation improves. How many times have you tied your goals to your finances? Maybe you have told yourself you will only further your education once you can afford to enroll yourself in a university or that you will only start looking for love once you can afford certain luxuries.

When you make your goals dependent on external circumstances, you create unnecessary delays. The Universe is waiting to help you, but only after you take the first steps to manifest your desired future. There will never be a "perfect time" to start pursuing your goals because life isn't perfect. You cannot wait to receive validation from your environment before you start making moves.

If you don't set goals, you won't know where you're heading. The lack of clear and actionable goals places you at a disadvantage before you even start. Why? Because you don't have any kind of plan anchoring your decisions. Goals help you make informed decisions that are targeted toward a certain outcome. This removes all kinds of delays or distractions which would typically eat away at your time. When you know where you are going, you are more likely to get there quickly. A life grounded in meaningful goals is never stagnant because the goals provide a continuous and steady motion forward.

Intentional Goal Setting

When you think about pursuing a goal, there is a natural tendency to imagine and place a lot of emphasis on the outcome. Imagining the outcome is motivating. The only problem with this approach is you forget to appreciate the journey. By not paying attention to the process, it becomes difficult for you to see how far you have come and the many ways you have transformed in pursuit of your goal. For me, the journey is the meaningful part in achieving my goals because it reveals parts of myself I had never known and teaches me valuable life lessons.

Intentional goal setting is all about shifting your focus from the reward of the finish line to the value in the process. Instead of imagining who you will be once your plans fall into place, you bring your attention to who you are as you make small changes to your life every day. This shift in perspective is key. When we focus on the outcomes of our goals, we tend to look at our lives from an outside-in perspective, as though we were an observer watching to see how our lives will develop over time. However, as soon as the focus becomes on the transformation happening here and now, at a micro level, we adopt an inside-out perspective on our lives and pay more attention to how our thoughts, emotions, and behaviors shape our reality.

Another beautiful aspect of intentional goal setting is how it demands we be truthful about our desires. Do you want a car to make it easier to get from point A to point B or do you want one because everyone in your circle of friends has one? If it's merely for transportation, does it matter whether it's a top of the line, brand new vehicle or a pre-owned vehicle in excellent condition? This also applies to other desires like owning a property or sending your children to a specific school. What is behind your desires? Do you secretly wish to impress people or are your goals rooted in intention?

In a magazine article I read once, a woman was devastated after receiving rhinoplasty surgery (commonly known as a nose job) and felt she couldn't recognize herself in the mirror. She mentioned that for many years, she wanted this particular procedure done. She'd seen how some of her female colleagues were given preferential treatment at work after undergoing the surgery. She thought it would help her get a promotion at work, or at the very least, help to get her noticed by her office seniors. Though the doctors did everything she asked, she wanted her old face back—even if it meant reversing the procedure. When asked what this would mean for her career development, the woman said, "I don't even enjoy what I do anyways!"

Take a moment to reflect on the times you have strived for a goal that you didn't truly desire. Perhaps you were influenced by your parents' wishes or the success of your friends and made a decision to pursue something you never wanted. Intentional goal setting puts a spotlight on the truth behind everything you want. It asks the question: Why are you pursuing this goal? Why are you making these lifestyle changes? If you find it difficult to justify a particular goal, I would invite you to examine the goal to figure out what might have influenced you to pursue it.

A good question to ask yourself when setting intentional goals is: How do you want your life to look five years from now? When answering this question, keep these three points in mind: Dream big, narrow down your goals, and create a plan. Below are just a few examples of big dreams:

- I want to have my own family.
- I want to be financially independent.
- I want to be successful in my career.
- I want to retire.
- I want to travel the world often.

Next, you will need to put your detective hat on and ask yourself why you want your life to look like this in five years. Remember to answer truthfully so that you can assess whether or not these goals are rooted in your heart's desires. If you cannot justify the need to accomplish some of your goals, you may need to trace where the desire to accomplish the goal began, who was involved, and the mental dialogue you had with yourself. Below is an example of examining the goal of starting a family:

I want to have my own family

- I want my own intimate circle of support.
- I am ready to love and be loved in return.
- I am financially stable.
- I love nurturing children.

When you can justify your goals and have a strong emotional investment in accomplishing them, you have a higher chance of seeing them through. This is because intentional goals are usually founded in purpose. You decide to accomplish something because of an inner longing or passion. Even when obstacles come along the way, your goals will remain anchored in a deeper part of who you are. If you are curious to know whether your current goals are founded in purpose, consider answering the following questions:

- Are your goals aligned with your core values and beliefs?
- Do your goals help you move forward in life?
- Are your goals rooted in a deep passion that you have?
- Are your goals an expression of who you are?

If you are interested about setting intentional goals but don't know where to start or how they would look, you can customize these five intentional goal ideas below to suit your own lifestyle:

Idea 1: Learn Something New

Have you considered going back to school to broaden your knowledge about a specific career field? Or learn a skill you have always dreamed of applying in your life? If this resonates with you, why not consider pursuing further education? Learning something new can motivate you to step outside of your comfort zone and gain new experiences in life.

Idea 2: Letting Go of the Past and Focusing on the Present

Another worthy goal is learning how to let go of the past and focus your mind completely on the present. Not only will this give you an opportunity to be more present in your current relationships, focus on your career, and make your health a priority, it will help you release unresolved negative emotions and beliefs that have made it difficult to enjoy your life.

Idea 3: Being More Generous

Many seem to think by being generous with their resources, they are becoming poorer. While sharing your resources with others might temporarily leave you with less, you gain much more by strengthening your relationship to your values and making yourself a positive figure in another person's life. Giving your time for example, helps you strengthen your relationships and sharing your money makes you feel positive about who you are. Finding ways to help those around you adds more value to your character and makes you a magnet for goodness.

Idea 4: Taking a Break from Social Media

In this digital age, taking a break from technology is a worthy goal. It's so easy to forget that face-to-face interactions are healthy when you are so used to seeing your friends and family over a screen. Social media can weigh you down, especially when you are bombarded with negativity or images that trigger your insecurities. Taking a few weeks or months off social media can help you ground yourself in who you are and reconnect you to your own path.

Idea 5: Start Journaling

Journaling is a wonderful opportunity to put your thoughts on paper. This can be helpful to people who are overthinkers or struggle to compartmentalize their thoughts. You can think of journaling as a form of therapy which helps you make sense of your inner life and reflect on how you are feeling every day.

Big Picture Goal Setting

Goal setting is most effective when you plan your goals in a manner that makes them seem achievable. Achievable goals provide you with a sense of empowerment because you know how capable you are of achieving them. Large and extravagant goals sound good when you rehearse them to yourself or envision them in your mind, but they provide very little guidance about where you should start or what you should focus on to achieve them.

Have you ever wondered how the world's richest men and women were able to accumulate so much wealth? Maybe some of their wealth had to do with having the right product at the right time, but it would be unfair to credit all of their success to pure chance. First, we can safely say they had a dream or a higher goal which they wanted to achieve. They must have aspired to be successful in their specific industries or crafts. Their aspirations carried a magnetic force, helping them find ways of progressing forward, one step at a time.

Some of those who have built billion dollar empires began their businesses with $0 in the bank, or a few thousand dollars if they were fortunate. Their immediate goal was to at least double their income, however, in the back of their minds, they were thinking about their bigger aspirations and goals. Every step they took was informed by what they need to do in the present moment to reach their future aspirations. Their minds were simultaneously in the present and in the future. Imagine the kind of focus it takes to make decisions that are not only valuable for your life now, but will also be valuable in 10 years time. Billionaire and founder of Microsoft, Bill Gates, was quoted saying about his tech company, "Microsoft was founded with a vision of a computer on every desk, and in every home. We've never wavered from that vision." (AZQuotes, 2021)

Goal setting strategies used by the rich and famous aren't a secret! If you are willing, you can also experience the benefits of planning your goals with the future in mind. The method I will explain to you is known as big picture goal setting or backward goal setting. It refers to the process of setting the ultimate dream or goal you intend on achieving and working backward, detailing all of the smaller goals and milestones you need to reach to achieve your higher goal. This process is useful because it allows you to focus on your immediate tasks which are actionable and realistic, and ultimately shape the future you desire. Below are four steps for setting and achieving big picture goals:

Step 1: Think of a Big, Broad, and Distant Aspiration or Goal

Think of a long-term goal you have that doesn't seem achievable in the near future. If you don't have a goal in mind, you can think of abstract wishes or aspirations you might have, like being prosperous in your career. It's important to start off with one goal or one aspiration and make it your focus. You don't want to overwhelm yourself juggling two different sets of tasks simultaneously. Lastly, make sure it's a goal or aspiration you deeply desire; ask yourself what accomplishing this goal would mean for you.

Step 2: Break Down Your Goal into Smaller Goals

Take a look at your big goal and write down four or five steps you would need to take to achieve it. Don't worry about whether you can implement these steps right now; in the next step, we will break these goals down into smaller targets. To illustrate how you would break down your big goal, I will use starting a business as an example. Below are five smaller goals that would help me achieve my bigger goal of starting a business:

1. Write a business plan.
2. Secure funding.
3. Find a location for the business.

4. Create a marketing plan.
5. Recruit a small team of staff.

Each of these five steps is crucial in achieving my big goal. Thus, I would have to treat them like individual goals and focus all of my attention and energy in making sure I successfully achieve all five steps.

Step 3: Split the Smaller Goals into a Number of Targets

These five steps give you direction and create various milestones you can look forward to along your journey. However, these smaller goals are still too big for you to take action immediately. For example, if I told you to write a business plan, where would you begin? When you split your small goals into even smaller targets, you can more simply focus on achieving each target to accomplish the goal. Once again, your attention is narrowed and your energy is directed at what you can do today to eventually reach your goal. Using the business plan example, I could set the following targets to reach my goal:

1. Figure out what kind of product or service you want to offer.
2. Decide whether the business will have a physical location or based online.
3. Determine the target market.
4. Create a sales strategy.
5. Determine whether the business idea is viable. If so, create financial projections.

There is no limit to the number of targets you can set, as long as each target is achievable and realistic. Setting a target like pitching to 1,000 investors simply isn't realistic and may put a lot of strain on you.

Step 4: Create a List of Single Actions

Even though it's possible to start implementing your targets today, creating a list of single actions will make completing targets much quicker. Look at each target and think of a list of single actions you can perform to help you achieve them. The aim here is to keep each single action short and specific. Depending on your lifestyle, you can choose how many single actions you want to perform each day or on your weekends until you complete a target. Below is an example of single actions I would take to determine a product or service for my business:

1. Research profitable business ideas.
2. Choose a niche business idea.
3. Research the pros and cons of starting up this business.
4. Find various products to sell within this business niche.
5. Choose a product with low overhead costs.
6. Find competitors who offer a similar product.
7. Think of ways to make your product offer better than your competitors.

Remember that your goals may change as time goes by. Be flexible enough to make adjustments to your single actions, targets, or smaller goals when necessary.

Remember that a change in your plans doesn't mean you have failed or that your ultimate goal is unattainable. Life is unpredictable and no matter how much work you put into planning, your plans may change. Don't let this discourage you; embrace your journey and learn how to celebrate the small victories.

Chapter 3: Health Is Wealth

The "health is wealth" proverb emphasizes the importance of taking care of our bodies so we can live disease-free and maximize the full potential of our minds. You'll notice I included mental well-being when talking about health. This is because a healthy mind fosters a healthy body, and vice versa.

The mind-body connection has been studied throughout a number of disciplines, from psychology to medicine. It explains how your physical health is intertwined with your mental and emotional health. Studies suggest that stressful emotions can negatively impact the body's immune system by changing the blood cell function. (Newport Academy, 2019) One study found that when people were stressed for a prolonged period of time, their bodies were slower to heal and vaccinations were less effective. (Newport Academy, 2019) While stressful emotions could lead to poor health, uplifting emotions were found to improve mental and physical health.

One study looked at the impact of the mind-body connection in breast cancer survivors. Researchers placed the breast cancer survivors into two groups: the first practiced mindfulness meditation and attended a support group while the second group did neither. The results of the study showed practices like mindfulness meditation and attending support groups could lower a survivor's stress levels. (Newport Academy, 2019) Researchers found a change in brain activity among those that meditated and attended a support group. Overall, this group had longer telomeres, which are protein complexes found at the end of chromosomes that protect against disease. Shorter telomeres, on the other hand, are linked to disease. (Newport Academy, 2019)

I once attended a seminar hosted by a successful business woman named Sam. The seminar was based on her own life story and how she learned the power behind the mind-body connection. Sam was a hard-working single mother of two who had recently graduated with her PhD and juggled running a successful mom-and-pop business while raising her children. When she shared details about her life, she seemed put together. She worked in the finance industry but left because she saw an opportunity to become an entrepreneur. Within three years, Sam was making six figures. This opened many doors for her to branch out into other investments.

The tradeoff she made to amass this level of success resulted in neglecting her health. Sam told me she went to bed around 4 a.m every night, only to sleep three hours before getting up to prepare school lunches for her children.. She didn't have an appetite in the morning, so instead of having a healthy breakfast, Sam would drink two cups of coffee. At work, she would leave the "Do not disturb" sign on the door and only leave her office for a short trip to the vending machine to refill on snacks. Her body was so affected by living on sugary foods and beverages, that she was eventually diagnosed with diabetes.

When speaking to her doctor about her diagnosis, her doctor mentioned that the unhealthy food choices played a part in contracting the disease. He also believed, however, that Sam's stressful lifestyle played an even bigger role. Sam's fast-paced lifestyle caused her to ignore the cues she was receiving from her body. If she was tired, she drank caffeine instead of taking a nap or getting to bed earlier. The doctor also explained how important sleep was for her well-being. He compared a lack of sleep to leaving your car running for an extended period of time. Eventually, the car's battery will die, and you won't be able to start or move your car. The body needs sleep to recharge, otherwise you become vulnerable to chronic stress and anxiety, diseases, or burnout.

Let's Get the Body Moving

Many people are under the false assumption that physical exercise is only suitable for dieters who want to lose weight or build muscle. Physical exercise is actually a tool people can use to keep their health in check. Diet or not, you have a responsibility to ensure your body is functioning at its optimal level. Physical exercise can do more for you than sitting on the couch. Below are some of the benefits of physical exercise:

- Increases muscle and bone strength
- Lowers blood pressure
- Boost the levels of good cholesterol
- Improves blood circulation
- Regulates body weight

Physical exercise can also improve your emotional well-being. Think about how you feel after completing a workout. The feel good sensations you experience come from your body. During and after your workout, your body releases chemicals known as endorphins. These endorphins travel to your brain and reduce the perception of pain. They are also responsible for making you feel good about yourself after the workout, as though you were riding on a natural high.

It's easy to see how beneficial it is to develop an exercise routine. Perhaps you have tried incorporating physical exercise in your lifestyle before and couldn t seem to make it "stick". The only way physical exercise becomes a permanent part of your lifestyle is if you commit to exercising frequently and consistently. Most people make two major mistakes when seeking to incorporate physical exercise in their busy lifestyles. First, they set the expectation too high. Someone who has never been to the gym before gets a gym membership and starts training like they are a bodybuilder. This person is doomed to fail because that kind of advanced training only comes after several months of gradually intense workouts.

When starting out, it's better to set the bar low but commit to exercising consistently. For example, dedicating 30 minutes per day, every day, to working out is better than having to skip a couple of weeks to recover from overly-intense workouts. The second mistake most people make is to perform physical activity they don't enjoy! Instead of making you feel good about yourself, it will make you feel as though you're being punished. If you don't enjoy the gym, find other forms of exercise, like swimming, dancing, taking a walk in your neighborhood, playing tennis, or taking kick-boxing lessons.

Another tip when making physical exercise a habit is to adopt a "go with the flow" attitude toward your workouts. You may have planned to go riding on your bicycle, but when the time came you didn't feel like getting out of the house. Find other forms of exercise you can do indoors to replace the activity you were supposed to do. You can watch a home workout video on YouTube, take a dip in the pool, do some gardening, or do a few household chores. When you're feeling discouraged to workout, you can also turn it into a social activity. Invite your family to join you on a walk, play outside with your children, or join a running or cycling club.

Pay Attention to What You Eat

People who have built a general level of self-awareness are able to discern their thoughts and feelings. It's easy for them to identify emotional triggers, like being surrounded by negative people, and choose to distance themselves from them. I always admire those who are able to get behind their minds. However, I wonder how many have been able to get behind the food they consume? How differently would your diet look if you were able to discern which foods were positively impacting your well-being and which weren't? Having the ability to see the impact your food had on your health would make you choose to eat cleaner and replenish on as many nutrients as you can.

Even though you cannot literally see where your food travels after you have swallowed it and how it behaves inside your body, you can see evidence of its effects on your moods and how your body functions over time. You don't need a doctor to tell you that good nutrition is the foundation of a healthy body; you can feel the physical effects of consuming good nutrition as opposed to unhealthy foods.

Hippocrates, the father of Western medicine, coined the phrase "food is medicine." (Holmes, n.d.) By this, he meant that people were able to heal their bodies or invite sickness by the kinds of foods they ate. He believed that if people ate wholesome, nutrient-rich foods, they wouldn't need to depend on synthetic medicine created in a laboratory.

When I think of our predecessors and how they would have cured themselves without being able to visit a doctor and get a prescription, I find myself leaning toward Hippocrates' argument that food is truly medicine. Our forefathers ate certain fresh fruits and vegetables to absorb the vitamins, minerals, and fibers. Not only would they use food to heal illnesses, they would also use food for energy, to boost their immune systems, and strengthen their muscles and bones.

If I were to go back in time, holding a typical fast food hamburger meal you'd find around the corner, to give to my ancestors to eat, they would look at the meal with a great amount of skepticism. First, they wouldn't recognize the hamburger meal as real food since it doesn't consist of whole, fresh ingredients. After picking it apart, they would probably eat the fries since carbohydrates provide a source of energy. After a few hours, however, their blood sugar would spike and they would feel sluggish and severely dehydrated.

Hippocrates believed that many of the diseases people suffered were due to consuming an unhealthy diet, with low to no nutrient-rich foods. He also believed the symptoms many diseases cause could be reversed when the patient committed to eating a balanced and healthy diet. I wonder what the father of Western medicine would say if he saw how throughout the world, diabetes, heart disease, and obesity were on the rise. A National Diabetes Statistics Report released in 2020 showed that 34.2 million U.S. citizens (just over 1 in 10 Americans) had been diagnosed with diabetes and 88 million American adults (1 in 3 Americans) had been diagnosed with prediabetes. (CDC, 2020)

There are four types of foods that greatly increase an individual's likelihood of being diagnosed with type 2 diabetes.

1. Highly Processed Carbohydrates

Do you remember those fast food fries I mentioned earlier? They are a good example of a highly processed carbohydrate. In essence, any food made from white flour, white sugar, or white rice falls under this category. These foods have been stripped of the fibers and minerals your body needs and consist mostly of calories. Since they are void of natural fibers, your body can easily digest them. This isn't good though, because the sugars from these foods are quickly absorbed in your blood and cause you to experience a high burst of energy, followed by a sharp decline. Regularly consuming highly processed carbohydrates can cause a spike in insulin levels, putting you at risk of eventually developing type 2 diabetes with repeated consumption.

2. Sugary Beverages

Regularly drinking sugary beverages, like fizzy drinks, sweet tea, and energy drinks, can put you at risk of developing type 2 diabetes, too. There are two main reasons for this. First, drinking sugary beverages may lead to excessive weight gain, which can spike your insulin levels. Second, the sugar load in these drinks may lead to an increase in insulin resistance. (Radcliffe, 2018) Because sugar is addictive, drinking sugary beverages instead of water can easily become a habit. If you crave a sugary drink, prepare a fruit smoothie instead, or make your own homemade lemonade or iced tea.

3. Trans and Saturated Fats

It's true that not all saturated fats are bad for you. You can fit saturated fats in two categories; healthy and unhealthy. Below is a list of healthy saturated fats:

- Whole eggs
- Cheese
- Avocados
- Nuts
- Chia seeds
- Extra virgin olive oil

It's important to note that even with these healthy saturated fats, you should limit them to less than 10% of your daily calorie intake. Trans fats like fried takeaway meals and processed foods, as well as unhealthy saturated fats, like fatty cuts of red meat, high-fat dairy products, butter, and coconut and palm oils, can increase your cholesterol levels. High cholesterol levels put you at risk of developing type 2 diabetes.

4. Red and Processed Meats

Both red meat and processed meats have been linked to type 2 diabetes. Some processed meats, like bacon, sausages, ham are particularly unhealthy because they contain a lot of sodium, which can increase your risk of high blood pressure. A study conducted in 2011 found that a three ounce serving of red meat per day (roughly the size of a deck of cards) increased a person's risk of type 2 diabetes by 19%, while an even smaller amount of processed red meat increased the risk to 51%. (Pan et al., 2011) Fortunately, there are so many other types of protein you can eat that don't carry such harmful side effects. Examples of these proteins include lean cuts of poultry, salmon, sardines, lean grass-fed beef, and ostrich.

Reprogramming the Reward Trigger

By thinking about what you choose to eat and changing your diet accordingly, you can reduce your risk of contracting illnesses related to unhealthy eating. Even people whose diets are largely based on takeaways or microwaveable foods can choose healthier alternatives without having to prepare fresh food from scratch. There are many healthy food options at sit-down restaurants and fast-food drive-throughs that you can substitute for high-calorie, high-carb options.

I understand how difficult it is to make good decisions for your internal body when you can't even see the seriousness of what your food does inside. When the signs show up, the damage is usually already done. I would like you to imagine your internal body is an engine which requires the correct type of fuel to function at optimum level. If you mistakenly put gasoline in a diesel car, you would cause serious damage to your car's fuel injection system. You would hear a loud knocking sound when accelerating, the engine warning light would come on, the exhaust would produce an excessive amount of black smoke, and the engine might completely shut down. Whenever you make unhealthy food choices, imagine similar side effects are occurring in your body's engine.

Human beings are driven by rewards. When we believe something is going to feel good, we are more likely to do it. For decades, advertisers have marketed fast food products as desirable, feel-good food. It's no wonder high-calorie, high-carb meals are widely known as "comfort foods". When we eat these foods, we feel nostalgic, warm, and consoled. Emotional eaters often binge on comfort foods to feel better about themselves and to dissociate from their strong emotions. Biology can explain why junk food makes us feel good. The brain naturally releases dopamine (a chemical which makes you feel good) whenever you eat. The release of dopamine when eating junk food, however, is more powerful than when you eat whole foods. Since the brain is hardwired to seek rewarding behaviors, eating junk food quickly becomes something a person craves or thinks about often. It's as if the brain is looking for the next "high" and easiest way to get it is from consuming junk food.

If your brain believes it is receiving a reward by eating unhealthy foods, quitting junk food won't be easy or straightforward. I have often heard people say, "Practice self-control and you will stop craving junk food" but in reality, the solution is far more involved. When your body is triggered to eat something unhealthy, your prefrontal cortex (the part of your brain associated with self-control) is the first to switch off. Your rational brain sleeps and the reward system in your brain is activated. This is why resisting temptation to eat junk food can feel painful. Your brain feels deprived of what it has perceived as "good."

I've spent many years investigating the best way to curb a bad eating habit when self-control isn't an option. My research led me to an ancient spiritual practice that's widely accepted in modern psychology:the practice of mindfulness. Mindfulness focuses on bringing your attention to what is here. There are so many activities occurring around you and within you right now as you read this sentence. Mindfulness values each present moment, as if it was all that you had. Embrace what is happening now. In the next chapter, I will share with you a mindfulness meditation exercise. For now, I would like to explain how mindfulness can help you combat an unhealthy eating habit.

Practicing mindfulness can help you get behind the "reward" triggering you to frequently eat junk food. It can help you figure out what's driving you towards unhealthy food, emotional eating, and using food to escape from your life . Once you see the underlying cause of your eating habit, you may understand why junk food has been a source of pleasure for so many years. You can even take it a step further and look into the behaviors you have deemed pleasurable over the years to figure out where they come from. A binge eater may find food pleasurable because their parents showed them love by buying them sweets and taking them to fast food restaurants as a child.

When you are aware of what triggers the reward, you can make the reward more positive. Instead of deriving pleasure from eating junk food, you can find a mentally stimulating hobby, like painting or playing a musical instrument. Make that your go-to whenever your brain craves junk food. Remember, the brain isn't particularly hooked on the unhealthy food choices, but more so on the "high" it receives from consuming them. Therefore, by finding a positive "high," you can still find ways to reward yourself without having to harm your body in the process.

Chapter 4: Leading Your Day on the Right Foot

When I was in community college, I met a classmate who was interested in developing his skills as an entrepreneur. He was studying toward his Finance degree and looked forward to opening his startup business. I was really inspired by this guy because of the passion he exuded when he spoke about the kind of changes he wanted to make in his community and the world at large. I gave him all the advice I could give and wished him well on his entrepreneurial endeavors.

A year later, I got a call from him. During the call he would tell me how he had spent the past year working on a business that was progressing at a snail's pace. He told me he was ready to quit and look for a job in the corporate world because he couldn't handle the pressure. I could sympathize with him because I had seen from watching other entrepreneurs that starting a business wasn't easy. I also knew this guy loved entrepreneurship and I couldn't stand to watch him quit. Instead of telling him everything was going to be okay, or that he was right to look for a corporate job, I decided to tell him this:

Whether you choose to quit or persevere through these present challenges, you are making a choice.

I knew he was under a lot of stress and that quitting would be the easier route. I also knew he would live with regret for the rest of his life if he did. When your mind and soul are in alignment to do something, you feel out of place or restless when you are not doing it. This is why people who have walked away from their purpose end up feeling depressed, undone, and joyless. The temporary choice to quit would take the pain away, but was that worth a lifetime of inner turmoil?

He had a chance to choose to persevere through the challenges. In the heat of the moment, persevering through a challenge doesn't seem like a choice anyone wants to take, but in hindsight, it is always the choice that leads to self-mastery. What's the worst that could've happened if he chose to spend a few more years working on his business? Perhaps he would stay at home longer, sacrifice spending time with his friends, or invest a lot more money in sustaining the business. If this was the risk it took for him to live a life aligned to his purpose, I still believe it would be worth it.

Every road you travel in life will have speed bumps. Those who are employed and unemployed experience obstacles. Couples who are dating and those who are married experience obstacles. If you live alone or live with your family, you will experience obstacles. Whether you are rich and have a portfolio of investments or living on the welfare system, you will experience obstacles. Once you have figured out what you want out of life and how you want to live it, choose to persevere on that path. The grass isn't greener on the other side.

Showing Up Early for Your Life

Many CEOs and celebrities have cited waking up early in the morning as one of their daily habits. They start their days before the sun has risen and use that time for getting a headstart at work or focusing on enriching activities, which help them get in the correct frame of mind. In the early hours of the morning, everyone in the home is asleep, the birds haven't begun chirping, and the streets outside are quiet. You are the only person awake and you have time to think clearly and set your intentions for the day.

I'm sure you're wondering "How early is *early*?" You are the only person who can set your body clock. Experiment with waking up at different times to see which hour feels comfortable for you. The CEO of Apple, Tim Cook, wakes up at 03:45 a.m and checks his emails before his colleagues wake up. Actor Mark Wahlberg wakes up at an even earlier hour—02:30 a.m.—to pray, exercise, and play golf. Oprah Winfrey, on the other hand, wakes up at 06:02 a.m. everyday to make time for reflection, exercise, and meditation.

Very few people will commit to waking up at 03:00 a.m. It also wouldn't be a healthy waking hour if you go to sleep later than 07:00 p.m.. However, waking up any time after 05:00 a.m. can help you get a headstart in your day and improve your overall productivity. There are a few strategies you can practice to help you get used to waking up a few hours earlier. The first is to open your curtains as soon as your alarm clock goes off. Natural light can help you wake up and signal to your brain it's time to get the day started. The second strategy is to get up from your bed and walk outside. If you have a garden or balcony, enjoy a cup of herbal tea outdoors and allow the natural elements of wind and sunlight to gradually wake you up. Lastly, you can also do a few light exercises to get your metabolism active. If you prefer not to exercise, you can do light stretches instead.

There aren't any known health benefits to waking up early, though there are a few other benefits which make waking up early a valuable habit to incorporate in your day. Below are five benefits to starting your day early:

1. You Set the Tone for Your Day

When you wake up early, you get to decide what kind of day you expect to have. You can think about all of the small goals you want to achieve by the end of the day, the people you want to contact, and the mood you wish to maintain. Get into the habit of setting positive intentions for the day by declaring what you hope to experience, feel, and achieve. For example, you can say "I intend on learning from other people. I intend on greeting every obstacle with confidence. I intend on seeing the best in other people. I intend on finding new ways to work efficiently" and so on.

2. You Aren't in a Rush

Have you ever missed your alarm and woken up late for work? The adrenalin from jumping out of bed, mindlessly taking a shower, forgetting to eat breakfast, and racing through traffic can leave you feeling grumpy and unfocused. When you wake up early, you aren't in a rush to get out of the bed. You can spend 15 minutes reflecting on the new day and another 15 minutes reading a chapter from a book. By the time you get to work, you have satisfied every personal desire that crept up in the morning and your mind can focus on the busy work day ahead.

3. You Can Enjoy Your Solitude

We live in a society where everybody is interconnected and constantly engaging with one another through technology or physical interactions. It can be very difficult to find time for yourself, especially if you live a very busy lifestyle. The mornings are a great time to spend in solitude. Everything around you is still and you can zone in on how you are feeling. You can also spend your quiet time asking yourself reflective questions about your career, health, and relationships. Think of it as an opportunity to review your progress and conduct a mini self-assessment.

4. You Catch the Sunrise

We tend to overlook the importance of sunlight, especially in improving our mood and making us feel lighter and happier about our lives. If you wake up late, you will miss the sunrise and probably won't have another opportunity during the day to sit outside and allow your skin to naturally produce vitamin D.

5. You Are More Aware of the Breakfast You Consume

A healthy breakfast is essential for providing your body with enough energy to make it through the morning. When we are in a rush, we grab a snack, coffee, or whatever we can get our hands on, without thinking about the nutritional value of our food choices. Waking up early gives you plenty of time to prepare a nutrient-rich breakfast and, if you're financially savvy, you will also have time to prepare your work lunch at home. You will also have plenty of time to savor your breakfast, eating slowly and noticing when you are full.

If you hope to adopt any kind of habit, you must be willing to practice the new behavior until your brain learns the pattern. If you aren't used to waking up early, the first few days may be very tough. Your brain probably associates sleep with pleasure and waking up early as a form of punishment. Therefore, be gentle with yourself in adopting this new behavior and keep your expectations low for the first few weeks. For instance, in the first week, you can start by waking up 15 minutes earlier than usual. In the second week, you would increase the time to 20 minutes and in the third week, increase it again to 25 minutes. Do this until you are comfortable with the new hour you choose to wake up.

Another tip for easing yourself into waking up earlier is to start sleeping earlier. You need about eight hours of sleep to wake up feeling rested. In other words, if you decided to wake up at 6 a.m., you would need to be asleep by 10:00 p.m.. Switch off all technological devices an hour before your bedtime. The light coming from your cell phone or TV causes your brain to stay up longer, making it hard to fall asleep. Instead of browsing through your phone or laptop, read a book, practice your positive affirmations, or go over your goals before you fall asleep.

It also helps to keep your alarm clock as far enough from your bed that you have to get up to turn it off. This will also ensure you don't hit the snooze button and go back to sleep. Lastly, you will need to make waking up early a reward. If you're feeling forced to wake up early, it will be hard for you to keep it going consistently. You must retrain your mind to consider waking up early something to look forward to. Find an activity you are really passionate about and schedule it in the mornings. This will make you look forward to waking up and performing the particular activity.

Creating a Morning Ritual

Making the most of your mornings matters because it sets the tone for your day. If you happen to have a chaotic morning, you may feel stressed and anxious throughout the day. The best way to control how your mornings flow is to create a morning ritual. Morning rituals are practices you perform to energize your body, mind, and spirit. These practices leave you feeling rejuvenated and ready to tackle the day ahead.

Morning rituals are not the same as morning routines. A morning routine may involve waking up, brushing your teeth, taking a shower, and eating breakfast. You perform these activities so many times that it becomes second nature. Your rituals may involve some of these activities, however, they should largely incorporate practices that carry a significant amount of meaning to your well-being. For instance, after performing a particular practice, like prayer, you feel grounded, focused, and empowered to make the most of your day. It becomes more than something you merely add on your to-do list. A good tip for selecting practices to include in your morning ritual is to ask yourself whether those practices energize you and make you appreciate your mind, body, and spirit.

Four Powerful Morning Rituals for a Productive Day

If you desire change in your life, it's important to wake up feeling like you can conquer the world every morning. Before opening your emails or social media accounts, you can take 15 to 30 minutes to perform a morning ritual that will set you up for success during the day. Morning rituals focused on increasing productivity give you an opportunity to choose a winner's mindset and organize your day before it even begins. Below are four morning rituals for a productive day:

Set Your Intentions for the Day

There's nothing worse than starting your day in a bad mood. Perhaps you read a heartbreaking message, fought with your partner, or entertained a negative thought about yourself. These uncomfortable events can leave you feeling discouraged throughout the day. By setting intentions even before you leave your bed, you essentially control how you would like your day to turn out.

Intentions are positive statements you declare or write down that condition your mind to think and feel exactly what you want it to. You can think of intentions as seeds you drop in your mind that grow into the kind of thoughts and feelings you desire. When setting intentions for the day, you can think of how you want to show up for others, your level of productivity at work, and the goals you want to accomplish for the day.

Your intentions can be as broad or as simple as you would like. For example, your intention may be as specific as saying "I intend on drinking eight glasses of water today" or as broad "I intend to show kindness to others." Starting your day with an intention will set the tone for how you wish to engage with other people and help you achieve the positive mindset you hope to carry throughout the day. If you are actively trying to break a bad habit, setting intentions for the day can help you focus your mind on the positive behaviors you want to perform. Below are a four steps showing you how to set intentions:

Step 1: Get Clear on Your Values

When setting intentions for the day, it's always good to get clear on your values. When you know what is important for you in life, you can create meaningful intentions that align with your beliefs. Someone who values punctuality would create an intention related to submitting work on time and someone who valued open-mindedness would create an intention related to learning new information.

Step 2: Get Clear on Your Desires

Have you ever thought about what you want from each day? This may be a difficult question to answer when your weekdays are full of the same activities. Each day, you can wake up and decide on the feeling you'd like to feel most. Do you need peace? Or a boost of confidence? Set your intentions on desired emotional states and allow your mind to manifest this experience.

Step 3: Set Your Intentions Before You Get Out of Bed

The best time to set your intentions is right when you wake up. Your brain hasn't fully engaged in deep cycles of thoughts, so your mind is clear and easily influenced. After waking up, take a few deep breaths and give yourself a few seconds to gather yourself. Place your hand on your heart or your belly (whichever feels natural for you) and declare your intentions, speaking on whatever arises for you in that moment.

Step 4: Focus on Your Intentions Throughout the Day

It's not enough to set intentions in the morning and forget about them. You need to constantly remind yourself about the kind of day you'd like to have. A good time to recall your intentions is when you have a moment to yourself during your work day. Find a quiet place to sit alone and assess how you are feeling and remind yourself of your desired emotional state. You can also schedule reminders on your phone to alert you at specific times of the day about the intentions you have set.

Practice Meditation

Incorporating meditation as part of your morning ritual can positively transform your life. Meditation helps you slow down and control your thoughts. You are able to bring your attention to each thought, then gently release it. This can be a powerful practice for those who work in highly stressful careers and have hundreds of thoughts flying through their minds each day. Instead of obsessing over a thought or allowing it to grow and become bigger than it ought to be, practicing meditation can give each thought the attention it deserves without letting it take over your focus. Below are three benefits of practicing meditation in the morning.

1. You Can Enhance Your Awareness

The mind has a tendency to jump from one thought to another without reaching any resolutions. Thoughts come and go as fast as it takes a monkey to jump from one tree to the next. This can cause you to overthink and get caught up in a loop of thoughts without a chance to clear your mind. Through your meditation practice, you can tune into your mind and body and become aware of your thoughts. You are able to see patterns of negative thinking and detach yourself from them. For instance, you would notice self-doubt but realize that it's only a feeling passing through your consciousness.

2. You Can Prevent Stress and Anxiety

One of the health benefits of meditation is how it can reduce stress and anxiety. Mornings can be stressful, especially when you don't particularly like your job or dread the long commute to work. Meditation allows you to make time for yourself and forget about all of your deadlines and obligations. Your meditation practice can slow your heart rate, increase your blood circulation, and release all sense of tension in your body. Beginning your day in a peaceful state of mind can help you let go of other stressors in your mind and feel optimistic for the day ahead.

3. You Can See the Bigger Picture

Practicing meditation allows you to detach yourself from your thoughts and feelings to see the bigger picture. It's natural for your mind to bring up past failures or worry about the future, but dwelling on the past or future won't improve your level of productivity in the present. When your mind is empty of distracting thoughts, you are able to bring your focus on pressing issues you can control. This allows you to solve problems creatively and learn lessons from your mistakes.

Mindfulness meditation focuses on being present in here and now. If you want to change your current routine and incorporate healthy habits, you will need to be present in your personal development journey. Regularly practicing mindfulness meditation can help you achieve emotional balance and improve your physical well-being. Below is a guided mindfulness meditation script you can practice each morning to reconnect to your mind and body.

> *Get in a comfortable position, sitting on a chair or on the floor, with your back straight and your shoulders resting. Uncross your legs and allow your arms to hang loosely in your lap. Close your eyes and bring your awareness to your breathing.*
>
> *Notice the natural rhythm of your breath coming in and going out. Follow each breath all the way in and stay with it as it slowly leaves you. Notice your breath passing through your nostrils, filling your lungs with air. Stay with your breath as it gently pushes out of your lungs, through your nostrils and leaves your body.*
>
> *As you breathe in, think to yourself, "I know I am breathing in" and as you breathe out, think, "I know I am breathing out."*
>
> *Thoughts will come in and out of your mind throughout your meditation. This is natural and expected. Acknowledge each thought as it passes through your mind, without judging it. After acknowledging the thought, let it go and continue to focus on your breathing and back to the present moment.*
>
> *As you breathe in, think to yourself, "I choose to stay in the present moment" and as you breathe*

out, think to yourself, "This is a wonderful place to be in."

Continue to focus on your breathing for as long as you would like, noticing the pace and intensity of each breath. Take a moment to notice the thoughts and feelings that arise in the present moment; acknowledge them and gently let them go. When you are ready to end the meditation, bring your awareness to your body, gently open your eyes, and proceed to another morning ritual or continue with the rest of your day.

Express Gratitude

Since I incorporated a gratitude practice in my morning ritual, I have seen noticeable improvements in my well-being. I have a greater sense of clarity, a deeper appreciation for my life, and less anxiety when things don't go according to my plan. A simple definition of gratitude is having an appreciation for the gifts that life has to offer. These don't have to be materialistic gifts, per se, but can also be abstract gifts, like the gift of peace. Practicing gratitude can improve your life by encouraging you to focus your attention on everything good happening in each moment.

How many times have you woken up in the morning and thought, "This is going to be a long day!" or "The traffic is probably terrible!" More often than not, we are hardwired to notice all of the inconveniences around us than the good life has to offer. Fortunately, this isn't our fault, since research finds that our brains are programmed to remember negative events a lot easier than positive ones. Psychologists refer to this as negativity bias. The human brain feels the impact of a negative rebuke stronger than it feels the pleasure of praise. This is why months after resolving an argument with a colleague, you will still walk into the office feeling defensive or vulnerable, or why you are more likely to think of what could go wrong instead of what could go right.

Therefore, practicing gratitude forces your brain to go against its normal routine and begin to see life in a positive way. It's no wonder research shows those who practice gratitude regularly have higher levels of positive thinking and lower levels of depressive thinking (Berleena, n.d.) It gives you an opportunity to build positive thinking patterns, which after a while, lead to positive behavioral patterns. For example, when a person who is grateful for their job wakes up, they are thankful for another opportunity to work. This positive association with work helps them work smarter and harder and improves their work relationships.

Take a moment to think about one thing you are most grateful for right now. It can be big or small. Close your eyes and focus on this particular thing, noticing how your body responds to this image in your mind. As you strengthen your ability to focus on what you're grateful for, your perspective on life will be brighter and you will also build mental resilience to help you through difficult times. The more you practice gratitude, the stronger the awareness of your thoughts and feelings will be.

Your gratitude practice can be as short or as long as you want it to be. To start, you can write three things in your gratitude journal you are grateful for that moment. You can either write these three things as bullet points or as three separate paragraphs. It also helps to be specific about what you are grateful for. For instance, instead of saying "I'm grateful for my family", you could say, "I'm grateful for how supportive my family has been while I have been studying for my exams." If you are grateful for your home, mention what it is about your home you are grateful for. Is it the first property you own? Does it have a beautiful garden? Is it close to work?

If you don't enjoy journaling, you can record audio clips of yourself answering the question. Save these audio clips under one file and refer to them whenever you need encouragement. Below are a few more tips on practicing gratitude every morning:

- **Don't quit.** There will be mornings where you feel like there is nothing to be grateful for. Even so, this isn't an excuse not to practice gratitude. Quiet your mind by practicing a meditative exercise and then try again to think of some gratitude items.
- **Feel it.** While mindfulness meditation is a ritual that energizes your mind, gratitude is a ritual which energizes your heart. You need to

feel what you're grateful for in addition to thinking about it. If you are grateful for your car, think about how life was like without it and the many ways having a car has made your life a lot easier.

- **Share it.** If you're grateful for having someone in your life, express it to them. Let them know how much you appreciate them. Expressing gratitude can improve the quality of your relationships in your personal and professional life.

Create Positive Affirmations

Daily affirmations are positive statements expressing specific goals as if they've already been completed. Even though affirmations may sound simple, they are powerful enough to impact your subconscious mind. Just as repeating negative beliefs about yourself can lead to mental illness, repeating positive affirmations about yourself can improve your emotional well-being.

Positive affirmations reprogram your mind to think more highly of yourself and your life. If you have specific goals you want to accomplish, positive affirmations can help you grow into the person you'd like to be. It's such an empowering feeling to know you can shape your future with every good thought you exalt above those that are negative and self-destructive. It's empowering to finally replace your "I can't" with "I can" and your fears with unshakable confidence!

There are two great times to practice saying affirmations during the day: in the morning upon waking up or at night before you go to sleep. When practiced in the morning, affirmations can increase your level of focus throughout the day and keep you feeling encouraged amidst conflict or sudden challenges. Positive affirmations create higher vibrations for peace and happiness by subconsciously pulling you toward the things you desire. You become a magnet for opportunities, friendly people, and money.

There are six rules for creating explosive positive affirmations:

1. Always start with the words "I am."
2. Write your affirmations in the present tense.
3. Keep your affirmations positive.
4. Make your affirmations short and specific.
5. Include at least one dynamic emotion.
6. Keep your affirmations about yourself, not others.

Below is an example of a positive affirmation following all six rules:

"I am falling in love with who I am"

Watch how you word your positive affirmations; even slightly negative suggestions can reduce their power. If you were to say "I am ready to quit smoking," it wouldn't really empower a shift in your subconscious mind. However, an affirmation like "I am free from the need to smoke" creates a different vibration that inspires a mental shift. It's also important to remember that positive affirmations differ from intentions. Intentions condition your mind to face the day ahead, while positive affirmations sow seeds into your subconscious mind to create a mental shift in behavior. Both practices are powerful in their own right, although they serve different purposes.

Below are 10 examples of positive affirmations to get you thinking about your own:

1. I am celebrating being alive.
2. I am attracting prosperity into my life.
3. I am emotionally present in all my relationships.
4. I am growing into a better version of myself every day.
5. I am living my heart's desires.
6. I am in perfect health. I love my body.
7. I am effectively communicating my needs and desires at work.
8. I am confidently expressing who I am.
9. I am grabbing every opportunity I see.
10. I am excited about where my life is going.

Part 2: Success

Some people interpret the meaning of success as the accumulation of wealth. For them, success is measured by career milestones, work achievements, promotions, the purchasing of assets, and expanding their investment portfolio. For these people to feel successful, they need to prioritize financial freedom.

Others see success as reaching a state of happiness, peace, or fulfillment in their lives. For these people, success isn't based on accumulating wealth, but on achieving personal goals, strengthening relationships with loved ones, and living a kind of life that feels most authentic to them. For these people to feel successful, they need to prioritize personal growth and finding ways to be a better version of themselves.

These two definitions of success share a common theme: the acceptance of change. No one has ever succeeded by remaining in their comfort zone, because the comfort zone doesn't have any room for change. If you want to be a better version of yourself, you will have to accept change. You will need to do some introspection and figure out which behaviors and actions you need to let go of to achieve the kind of personal growth you want. Likewise, if you want to excel in your career and increase your bank balance, you will need to make adjustments to your lifestyle, expose yourself to new experiences, seek higher level knowledge, start networking, work longer hours, and so forth.

Everybody wants success, but a few are willing to make the changes that need to be made to achieve their desires. Making these changes is just a small price you have to pay to live the kind of life you envision. Change is a necessary part of success. In the long run, you will thank yourself for your courage.

Chapter 5: Making the Most Out of Your Daily Grind

You will spend a third of your life at work. That's a total of 90,000 hours spent on your daily grind over the course of a lifetime. (Vaughn, 2018) This statistic wouldn't be as shocking if everyone enjoyed the kind of work they do. Gallup conducted a global poll showing that out of the world's billion full-time workers, only 15% of people were engaged at work, meaning that 85% of people were unhappy with their jobs. (Clifton, 2017) If most of your time is spent at work and you are unhappy with the kind of work you are doing, is it possible to succeed in your career?

Some enjoy their jobs but cannot stand the work culture in their office. Maybe they have a strained relationship with their boss or feel betrayed by their colleagues, which impacts their level of productivity and reduces their work morale. When you work in an organization that weighs you down and makes you dread waking up every morning to go to work, succeeding in that environment will be difficult.

The best case scenario? You LOVE what you do. Waking up each morning to go to work should feel pleasurable, not painful. You should leave the office feeling like you still have energy in your tank, not running on low reserves. Your work should inspire you to dream big, study more, learn new skills, and accumulate wealth. If a third of your life will be spent on your daily grind, you should be working in an industry or career field that ignites your passions and aligns with your life's purpose. We've been told the main purpose of a job is to pay the bills, but I beg to differ.

The main purpose of a job is to guide you closer and closer to who you are and help you live a kind of life that feels authentically yours. Of course, everyone desires a comfortable life, however, this shouldn't be at the expense of your peace of mind. A highly stressful job you don't enjoy isn't worth the generous paycheck it comes with. Ideally, you should love what you do and feel as though your contributions at work are making a difference to your organization and in the lives of the customers you serve.

How To Love What You Do

There's an old saying that goes, "Do what you love and you'll never have to work another day in your life." When you're truly passionate about what you're doing, you won't feel like you're working. Creativity will come naturally and you'll have enough energy and focus to concentrate for longer hours and carry you through the day.

The main factor that allows you to fall in love with the work you do is finding purpose in your job. When President John F. Kennedy paid a visit to the NASA space center in 1962, he noticed a janitor who was carrying a broom. He excused himself from the people he was with, walked over to the janitor, and said "Hi, I'm Jack Kennedy. What are you doing?" The janitor responded, "Well, Mr. President, I'm helping put a man on the moon."

Even though the man was a janitor, cleaning floors and making sure the space center looked good, he found a lot of purpose in his role. He thought of himself as part of a bigger system, helping NASA complete its space missions. The sense of purpose he found in his job made him carry his job title with pride and do an exceptional job with the tools and resources he had. The small number of people around the world who love what they do, don't need to be encouraged to go to work or perform to the best of their abilities. They are naturally driven to excel at everyday tasks and make the most of the opportunities presented to them at work. As a result of this, they end up succeeding at what they do and going further to achieve greatness. Below are four strategies to help you learn how to do what you love:

1. Focus On What You Love

Before you can do what you love, you need to know what you love to do! What gets your heart rate beating faster when you talk about it? What subject can you read numerous books and articles about? What kinds of discussions are you an expert in debating? Finding what you love will show you where your passions lie. Even if you don't have the skills in that particular field, your passion will give you enough drive to study a course on it or receive your qualifications. Another way of finding what you love is by focusing on your values and personal strengths. There's a reason you have the kinds of beliefs and attitudes about life that you do. Determine what living a life of purpose looks like for you and how you could potentially turn that into a career.

2. Get Connected

When you're trying to find what you love to do, it's good to network with people who are already working in that field. Use sites like LinkedIn to identify people with job roles you want and connect with them. Engage with their content, ask questions, and take in what they have to say. Other ways of connecting with people is through following their channels on YouTube, their podcasts, or other platforms where they share valuable information. (some professionals may have websites and blogs) The aim here isn't necessarily to make friends, although it's wonderful if this naturally happens. By connecting with people that do what you love, you will be gaining insider knowledge into the field and what it takes to be successful in that role.

3. Develop Positive Habits

Many people cannot afford to quit their day jobs and pursue their passions. Positive habits help people stay committed to doing what they love, especially when their projects or plans are still side hustles. If you were to wake up and realize you were passionate about law, for example, you would need to develop positive habits to keep you focused on your law studies while waking up and going to work every day. You would also need to develop positive professional habits, like joining law societies and attending seminars to improve your skills. When you practice your positive habits regularly, they will keep you going, even when giving up seems easier.

4. Appreciate Your Mistakes

After finding what you love, you may begin to see your current career as a mistake. The truth is, if it wasn't for your current career, you wouldn't realize how much you desired change or growth. Every step of your journey is ultimately leading you to the kind of future you desire. Learn to embrace seasons of difficulty and learn the lessons that each experience comes with. See challenges as sources of information, telling you what's going wrong and needs your attention. If you cannot quit your current job immediately, find alternative ways of engaging in your passions after work or during weekends. Who knows? Maybe one day your side hustle will become your main hustle.

Dealing With the Pressure of Succeeding at Your Job

We will all make mistakes along our career paths on our road to becoming successful. These mistakes may sometimes lead to career delays, missed opportunities, suspension from work, or mental breakdowns. Climbing the corporate ladder isn't easy, especially when there's a lot of pressure on your shoulders to perform, meet targets, or work longer hours.

Some say "Pressure makes diamonds," but when you're caught up in the moment, pressure can make you think about quitting your job. It may cause you to feel like you've reached a roadblock in your career that's impossible to overcome. The trick when it comes to coping with pressure is to remain resilient. Hang in there a little while longer until the pressure subsides and you're able to think of solutions to current problems. Being resilient will help you stay flexible through challenges, making the necessary adjustments so you can quickly recover and spring back into shape.

You also need to understand yourself and how you cope with stress. Think about your typical go-to behaviors when you are feeling overwhelmed. If they are self-destructive, you have an opportunity of replacing them with healthier habits that will uplift your spirit during difficulties. If you don't have go-to behaviors, it may be useful to write down a few post-it notes and refer to them when you are feeling stressed. For example, you could write down "I will listen to my favorite song when I'm feeling stressed," and stick your post-it note somewhere around your office desk where you can see it or easily access it.

In the spirit of writing things down, it may be useful to write down everything that's causing you pressure. By writing down your stressors, you release the heavy mental load on your mind. It also gives you the opportunity to take action on some or all of these stressors, since you can easily identify them. If you can't fix your stressors right now, write down small tasks you can start implementing to gradually solve the problem. For instance, if you are feeling pressure to earn a certain amount of money from your career by a specific period, but don't have an immediate solution, you can find ways of "upskilling" yourself to adopt new skills and potentially attract new opportunities.

Successfully dealing with the pressures from your career requires a positive mindset. A positive mindset can reverse negative self-talk and make you see your situation as being less fearful or threatening than your mind imagines it to be. If you received an angry email from your boss, your mind could run wild thinking about the worst case scenarios that might follow. A positive mindset helps you see your boss as human first and accept that sometimes he or she may be angry, and that's perfectly normal. Your boss's anger isn't a reflection of you as a person or your capabilities at work. Once both of you have calmed down, you can schedule a meeting to discuss the dispute and reach mutual understanding.

When you adopt a positive mindset, you realize that it's not the end of the world when things don't go according to plan. Every problem has a solution and after a few months, you probably won't remember some of the stressors weighing you down right now. Learn to be patient during uncomfortable situations, knowing that eventually they will pass. Instead of focusing on what's going wrong in your work or private life, think about all of the things going right for you. There are some challenges you cannot control and instead of trying to fix them, simply let them unfold.

Creating a healthy work-life balance can help you reduce the pressure that comes from your job. A work-life balance is an equilibrium where a person focuses on the demands of their work as much as they focus on the demands of their personal life. Two factors which may hinder your work-life balance is working in a highly stressful and demanding job or having increased responsibilities at home. Ideally, you want to be able to give equal amounts of energy to your job and home life without reaching burnout. Every person's work-life routine will be different, depending on the demands of their job, whether they have children, or how much time they spend at work.

There's no such thing as the "perfect work-life balance," since balance isn't achieved in a day or a week, but over a long period of time. Instead of striving for a perfect work-life balance, strive for a realistic one that accommodates the demands placed on your life. Below are five tips for maintaining a healthy work-life balance:

Tip 1: Focus on Your Strengths

You cannot be all things to everyone at one time. Focus on what you're good at and outsource help for other tasks. For example, if you are a new business owner and aren't great with graphic design, outsource a freelance designer to help you create beautiful content.

Tip 2: Use Your Time Wisely

If you have a long to-do list with 20 tasks for the day, start with tasks that are most urgent and end with those which are not as urgent. If you like, you can also group your daily tasks under the following categories:

- Urgent and important
- Important but not urgent
- Urgent but not important
- Neither urgent nor important

Tip 3: Know Your Productive Times

Are you a morning person or a night owl? Understanding your most productive times of the day will help you organize your daily tasks. If you are a morning person, you can complete your urgent work tasks then so that in the evenings, you are focused on relaxing or spending quality time with your pets or family.

Tip 4: Make Time for Yourself

In the midst of work and your private life, you need to make time for yourself. I am a fan of having regular check-ins during work hours, where you find a quiet place to take a few deep breaths and assess how you are feeling. If you are someone who works a high- stress job, dedicate your weekends to your hobbies or relaxing social activities.

Tip 5: Organize Your Workspace

What's on your work desk right now? Stacks of paper and files that don't serve any purpose? If you work in a job where you spend most of your time sitting at your desk, you need to ensure you are comfortable and have all of the equipment necessary to work efficiently. Switch to a comfortable chair with back support, an ergonomic keyboard, a stand for your laptop, and so forth.

Achieving and Maintaining Financial Freedom

From a very early age, we are groomed for a life of independence. Our parents take us to school so we can learn valuable skills to help us secure jobs. However, the reality of life after school isn't as straightforward or easy as it seems. There are many college graduates sitting at home with degrees, unable to find work, or others that are working in low-earning jobs who struggle to make ends meet every month. While being dependent isn't an option once you become an adult, achieving financial independence is something many seek, but don't have.

Financial freedom is the ability to sustain your desired lifestyle without relying on a regular paycheck. In other words, when you are financially free, you no longer have to trade your time for money, like many people who work regular 9-to-5 jobs. There are three stages to becoming financially free. Perhaps you can envision yourself fitting into one of these categories:

Stage 1: No Financial Freedom

Most people begin at this stage. In order to earn a living, many people find employment and exchange time for labor. Since they are not financially free, they tend to live from paycheck to paycheck.

Stage 2: Temporary Financial Freedom

To reach stage two, a person must spend less than they earn and generate a pool of savings. They might save a portion of their income in savings accounts or invest in stocks or other securities. Many people who have reached this stage also have side businesses they run to generate a second stream of income. The higher their savings, the more their freedom grows. Eventually, they will have enough money to plan holidays, invest in their side businesses, contribute to their emergency fund, and so on.

Stage 3: Permanent Financial Freedom

A person reaches permanent financial freedom when their non-employment income exceeds their total expenses and they no longer need to exchange their time for labor. Many people who reach this point quit their daily jobs and focus their time on their side businesses or managing their investment portfolios. Others choose to retire at this stage. The best part is they have a choice of what to do with their time, money, and efforts; a privilege many people do not have.

The ability to make choices without thinking about whether you can afford something or not is true financial freedom. However, to reach it, we need to have a solid plan. Many dream of winning the lottery, but according to Mega Millions, the odds of an American winning the jackpot are one in 302.5 million. (Huddleston, 2021) You need to be practical when it comes to achieving financial freedom, and the best way to do that is to think of reaching financial independence as winning small victories over time. Focusing on each small victory will make the journey less overwhelming and more achievable. Remind yourself that every wise savings decision puts you a step closer to your financial freedom.

If we were to think of small victories worth celebrating along the path to financial freedom, we would certainly think of these:

Victory: Recovering from Financial Dependency

If you were financially dependent on someone else, you were most likely unsatisfied with your financial position. Your income was always capped to the budget given to you. Recovering from financial dependency is a small, yet phenomenal victory! Even if you haven't reached stability as yet, you are still one step closer to financial freedom.

Victory: Being Financially Solvent

When your expenses are lower than your earnings, you are financially solvent. This means that every month, you will be able to fulfill your financial commitments, pay off debt, and still have money left in your bank account. Even though you might not have any savings stashed away, you are able to live a comfortable life.

Victory: Having Financial Security

If you have a back-up plan like an emergency savings fund or a second source of income, you have financial security. In essence, even if you were to get fired from your job, you would still be able to survive on your second source of income or on your investments. Once you have reached financial security, you can begin building wealth.

Achieving financial freedom is a long-term goal that requires you to maintain positive financial habits which will keep you accountable and focused on spending less and saving more. Below are five positive financial habits you should incorporate in your lifestyle to make your road toward financial freedom more enjoyable.

1. Set Life Goals

Setting life goals will help you understand what financial freedom means to you. Having a general answer to why you desire financial freedom won't motivate you enough to make the hard and necessary changes to how you manage your money. Take a moment to think about how much you have in your bank account right now and the kind of lifestyle this entails. Think about what you can and cannot do right now because of your limited funds. Now fast forward to the future and imagine the kind of lifestyle you desire to live. In what ways is it different from how you're living now? Let your visions for the future help you set specific goals and milestones to get there.

2. Create a Budget

If you aren't used to living on a budget, this might be an uncomfortable lifestyle adjustment for you. Budgets aren't meant to be strict and rigid. They are meant to offer you enough money to live a modest lifestyle while putting the rest of your money in savings. If you stick to your budget, your bills will be paid every month and your savings will be on track. A budget will also help you become aware of frivolous spending so you can make the necessary cuts in what you buy.

3. Pay Off Credit Cards

Before you can start saving money, make sure you have paid your credit cards in full. Because credit cards come with high-interest, they are detrimental to your wealth building efforts. Since student loans, mortgages, and similar loans come with much lower interest rates, you can continue to pay them off gradually over time. However, ensure all of your debt is paid on time so you can improve your credit score rating.

4. Create Automatic Savings

Find ways to save money passively. For instance, you can match your employer's contribution to your retirement plan; this will immediately deduct your contribution before you receive your paycheck. You can also create an automatic withdrawal to your emergency fund or an automatic deposit to a brokerage account to buy shares every month.

5. Negotiate Everything

Many Americans are hesitant to negotiate prices from service providers. Of course, there are some items you cannot negotiate, like goods in a supermarket, however, if you are looking for a handyman or are ready to buy property, negotiating can save you a lot of money. Small businesses in particular tend to be open to negotiations, especially those offering discounts for bulk purchases. If you cannot find a good deal, look for businesses offering items on sale.

Four Strategies for Generating Multiple Sources of Income

Generating multiple streams of income leads to a greater amount of financial security. It's become difficult to rely on one source of income nowadays, especially because job security is not 100% guaranteed. When you have multiple sources of income, you don't rely on one source of revenue, which also ensures you always have money coming into your bank account. If you want to increase your sources of income and achieve financial security, there are four strategies to consider:

1. Diversify Your Investments

Diversifying your investments refers to investing in different types of assets to spread your risk and increase your chances of making money. Instead of taking $1,000 and putting it all on one stock, you can divide it into chunks and invest in several types of stocks, in different categories. However, any kind of investment is risky and there's a possibility you will lose money too. Once you have accepted the potential risks you can create a diversified portfolio. You can start by opening a brokerage account and investing in ETFs or mutual funds. Or you can invest in peer-to-peer lending companies, like Lending Club.

2. Sell Something

A great way to add an extra income stream is to sell something. By offering a product or service you could start a small side business that doesn't interfere with your daily grind. In business, these are referred to as passive income business, since the business generates money without too much involvement from the business owner. The best type of business to open is a home-based or internet-based business that won't require a lot of overhead expenses.

3. Start a Passion Project

Find something you are really passionate about and identify ways of making money from it. Perhaps you love cooking and can write various cookbooks to sell online. The options are endless when it comes to monetizing your passions, but one thing is for sure, there are at least a few hundred people on the internet at any given moment who share the same passions as you and would love to be a part of your project.

4. Invest in Property

Real estate is still one of the best investments to go into. Even though life as a landlord involves maintaining your property while supervising tenants, revenue from real estate can lead to a life of financial freedom. If you don't want to own real estate, you can invest in a REIT (Real Estate Investment Trust) or invest money in a real estate crowdfunding website like Fundrise. If you already own property, you can consider renting out a spare room, like an unused guest bedroom. Those who are fortunate enough to have large backyards can build an Accessory Dwelling Unit (ADU), which has its own separate entrance and exit, for tenants or short-term renters.

Passive Income Business Ideas

If you read stories of how many entrepreneurs accumulated their wealth, you'll notice a pattern: most of them made money from multiple streams of income. Similarly, the best investors know it's never a good idea to have all your eggs in one basket. By having income coming in from many different channels, entrepreneurs and investors can rest assured they will never dry out of money.

When increasing your income streams, it's important to avoid the allure of get-rich-quick schemes. There are so many of them marketed on the internet, stealing thousands of dollars from innocent people. There's no such thing as "easy money" or shortcuts to building wealth. If this was true, everyone would be wealthy. Many business owners choose to open passive income businesses as a way to add another stream of income. Even though these passive businesses are less labor intensive and require very little maintenance, business owners still need to invest money and their expertise in making them profitable.

Most internet businesses are passive, but business owners still need to build the digital infrastructure, create content, update the infrastructure every so often, and have an ongoing marketing budget. Don't think starting your own passive income business will be easy. Indeed, the potential to make thousands of dollars per month exists in most passive businesses, but you will need to put effort into making it work. Here are a few passive income business ideas to get your creativity flowing:

1. Start a Blog

It takes time to build a blog, get a community of subscribers and make money from selling ad space, although in the long run, the payoff is huge! The best time to get started with blogging is NOW because you need all of the experience and exposure you can get. Don't let your doubts get in the way; simply find a niche you're passionate about speaking or writing about and create meaningful content people would love to read.

2. Create an Online Course

You don't need to have a PhD to transfer your skills to paying online students. Being knowledgeable in a particular subject matter is all you need. Nowadays, people don't have the time or money to attend college or complete their degrees. They rely on online teachers to share valuable knowledge about various subjects, at a fraction of the cost. From creating one online course, you could earn revenue continuously for many years to come. Think about a subject you can speak about for hours and find ways of turning what you know into a meaningful course.

3. Buy and Sell on eBay

Online businesses are considered passive because your customer can be anywhere in the world, making a purchase while you are fast asleep. If you have products you want to sell, create an eBay account and advertise them to willing buyers. You can buy products at a discounted price and resell them at a markup. Figure out what you are interested in selling or buying and create a store specializing in that product. Your product could be antiques you found at a yard sale or pre-owned electronics that are in good working condition. The best part is you can sell your products from the comfort of your couch without having to rent out shop space.

4. Create an eBook

Similar to online courses, eBooks are educational or informational products which transfer skills, wisdom, and useful insights from the author to the reader. If you are comfortable writing long articles, you can think of eBooks as being a series of long articles merged in one product. Once again, pick a niche and write about a topic your audience wants to learn about. Look for trending search keywords and find out what people are curious to learn nowadays.

The Secret Wealth Formula

Did you know there is a secret formula for building wealth? This formula has existed for hundreds of years and is only practiced by extremely wealthy individuals. The secret wealth formula outlines the components necessary for wealth generation. Below is what the formula looks like:

$$M + K + S + A = W$$

The formula mentions four critical stages you need to go through before you can generate a significant amount of money. These stages are:

Stage 1: Mentality

Stage 2: Knowledge

Stage 3: Strategy

Stage 4: Action

The plus sign in between each stage indicates that you would need to successfully accomplish one stage to reach the next. Missing or neglecting a stage will hinder your wealth building progress and cause unnecessary delays. For example, you could acquire a wealth mindset and learn everything you need to know about investments and finance, however, if you don't have a plan or if you fail to take action, all of the preparation would be for nothing. Therefore, it's important to focus on learning as much as you can from each stage and developing the correct skills, rather than worrying about the amount of time it takes to complete a stage and move on to the next one. If you're ready to practice the secret wealth formula, consider the stages you will need to follow:

Stage 1: Wealth Mentality

Before you see millions of dollars in your bank account or investments, you need to see millions of dollars in your mind. Reprogramming your mind is the first step to generate wealth because you can only go as far as you can see. If you grew up being told money is too difficult to accumulate or that only a few people can ever become rich, it will be tough for you to identify wealth-creating opportunities. If you intend on making a lot of money, you need to believe it's possible for you to do it. Many of the world's richest men and women didn't come from privileged backgrounds, but they were convinced that if they worked smart enough, they could change their lives around and accumulate wealth.

A wealth mentality is one where you see abundance all around you, instead of lack or scarcity of resources. Even if you don't have money now, you are convinced that money-making opportunities exist and you have access to these opportunities. When you see abundance all around you, you are more fearless in making big decisions and traveling on paths few would travel on. You are more likely than the average person to think of an idea and implement it to see how far it takes you in your wealth building efforts.

The founder and CEO of Amazon, Jeff Bezos, saw that brick and mortar bookstores could only hold a limited amount of books due to the space available in the shop.

He took this limitation and turned it into a billion dollar business by offering a catalogue of online books, available for download anywhere in the world. (as long as the customer had a stable internet connection) How did Bezos demonstrate a wealth mentality? He turned a problem into an opportunity by creatively finding a broader solution that would increase the supply and demand of books.

Stage 2: Wealth Knowledge

It's nearly impossible to become an expert at anything without acquiring the specific knowledge to broaden your understanding in that particular thing. Everybody has a little bit of money but only those who study finance and business can generate billions of dollars. Think of wealth building as a craft. You need to invest time learning about it to solve financial problems in your life and gear yourself toward financial freedom.

On a personal level, you need to be knowledgeable about your own finances and develop healthy financial habits so you can spend less and save more. On a broader level, you need to be knowledgeable about the economy, financial investments, credit, interest rates, and other financial factors which will directly cr indirectly impact your wealth-building efforts. Lastly, you will need to learn a few valuable financial skills, like interpreting financial statements, learning how to diversify your investment portfolio, and applying effective investment strategies.

Stage 3: Wealth Strategy

Creating a wealth strategy is incredibly important, yet many people either forget to do it or cannot seem to find the value in it. Creating a wealth strategy includes coming up with clear and realistic financial goals and designing the best plan to reach them. Remember to put a time frame on achieving your financial goals so you know how much time you have to either save money or wait until your investment matures. If you are also considering retiring early, you will need to create a separate early retirement plan which would show you how much money you need to put away every month to retire at a specific age.

Stage 4: Wealth Action

Stage four ties all of the other stages together and gets you started on your wealth building journey. Without completing the above steps, your bank balance or investment portfolio will not grow. There's only so much learning and planning you can do before you need to put what you've learned and strategized to practice. Taking actions will also help you identify gaps in your learning or gaps in your strategy, which you can adjust quickly and continue moving forward.

This secret wealth formula isn't a magic trick that produces wealth at the flick of a wand. You play a crucial role in grabbing the opportunities available to you and turning them into profitable income streams. This happens gradually, depending on how consistent you are in working smart and making your money go further.

Chapter 6: Me Time

How much time do you spend sitting by yourself or doing an activity alone every day? A recent study showed the average American spends only 43 minutes by themselves each day. (Sadlier, 2019) This means daily distractions like work, social media, social events, partners, and children can steal away alone time. Time with yourself is just as important as the time spent with your closest family and friends. When you spend time with yourself, you learn about your own thought and emotional processes and realign with your goals. People who prioritize "me time" tend to have a greater level of self-awareness because a good portion of their time is spent introspecting. Understanding who they are gives them a greater sense of control over their behaviors and actions, which can also help to break bad habits and replace them with good ones. Below are other benefits of having "me time":

Me Time Helps You Destress

Having time to yourself gives you an opportunity to clear your mind and let go of overwhelming thoughts. For a moment, you remove yourself from everything else, like your work or your friends, and you have a chance to sit back and recollect yourself. Me time helps you destress because it breaks the cycle of overthinking and helps you put your life in perspective.

Me Time Teaches You How to Be Independent

When you are alone in a room reading a book, for example, there are no external influences or distractions competing for your attention. You can hear your thoughts and connect to your emotions without someone else informing what you should think or feel. Usually, the less time a person spends alone, the more uncomfortable they are with their own silence. Me time helps you appreciate your own company and shows you that you can source all of the happiness and joy you need from yourself.

Me Time Makes You More Creative

Spending time alone makes you more creative because you are free to think outside of social constructs. You can think broadly and envision your dreams. This helps you in brainstorming and planning your future career, financial health, and relationship goals.

Setting Up Your Own Reward System

You might feel motivated to pursue your goals diligently at first, but as time goes on, your motivation will wear thin and you'll need to have a reward system put in place to prevent you from delaying your progress. A good reward system gives you a reason to pursue a goal and complete it. Many times, the reward is something you deeply desire, which makes getting started on your goal that much easier. There are three steps you can follow in setting up a good reward system that helps you stay motivated.

Step 1: Break Down Your Goals

The first step when setting up a reward system is to create smart goals, then break them down into smaller goals and milestones. Breaking down your goals makes them more achievable and keeps you accountable to smaller actionable tasks.

Step 2: Track Your Goals

Without tracking your goals, you won't know if you have achieved them yet. Tracking your goals can be as simple as creating measurements or key performance indicators (KPIs) to notify you when you've accomplished what you set out to achieve. For example, if you wanted to lose weight, your KPI may be dropping a dress size. When your current clothes become too big, you would have evidence to show that you've reached a milestone. The tracking in itself is a reward because of how good it makes you feel when you can cross off a goal on your list.

Step 3: Choose the Right Rewards

After reaching a milestone, you will have the opportunity to reward yourself for your hard work. A few considerations need to be made when choosing a reward. First, you need to assess whether the reward counteracts the progress toward your goal or keeps you in alignment with it. If your goal is to lose weight, rewarding yourself with greasy takeout food would be counterintuitive. The better choice would be rewarding yourself with a new pair of jeans or booking a spa treatment.

Second, you need to assess whether the reward is something you can afford to give yourself often. Since you will have many milestones throughout your journey, it's important to make your rewards small enough so you can repeatedly reward yourself without spending too much money in the process. Oftentimes, the best gifts are those which can't be bought, like spending time with family or taking a walk in nature.

When you have created a reward system, ensure you only reward yourself once a milestone has been accomplished. Make rewards feel like special events so your mind constantly seeks after them. Moreover, don't make your rewards activities you do on a regular weekend, but rather exclusive activities you have reserved for when you make significant progress on your goals.

Making Time for Simple Pleasures

It's good to reward yourself whenever you reach a significant milestone, however, milestones don't occur every day. You can find alternative ways of making yourself feel good or maintain happiness every day by focusing on the simple pleasures of life. What are the simple pleasures of life? These are the often overlooked experiences that occur every day, which have the potential to bring about a lot of happiness, peace, and sense of fulfillment in your life.

For example, paying attention to a person's smile or enjoying the sound of their voice is a simple pleasure that can make you feel positive emotions, especially when the person is someone you love. You don't need to do too much to access these positive emotions, but to simply pay attention to what you are experiencing in this moment. Activating your sense of sight, smell, touch, hearing, and taste can also help you tap into the feel good emotions and experiences occurring in this moment. For example, if you come home to a delicious home cooked meal, you may feel happier and lighter. As an exercise, write down five positive emotions you feel throughout the day from doing regular household or work tasks. At the end of the day, reflect on how amazing these tasks made you feel.

The one notable threat to experiencing the simple pleasures of life is hedonic adaptation. Hedonic adaptation is when a once-pleasurable experience becomes less pleasurable over time. After eating the same home-cooked meal five days in a row, it stops becoming as pleasurable as it used to be. If you practice good self-awareness, you can easily pick up on the daily tasks that aren't as pleasurable as they used to be for you and find ways of switching them up. For example, instead of preparing chicken in the same way every day, you can prepare it differently each day and change how the meal looks and tastes. The more you rely on a pleasurable activity, the less of an appeal it will have for you in the long run. Be ready to switch things up and find alternative ways of making yourself happy when your regular routine starts feeling bland. Below are 20 suggestions of activities you can do to get more pleasure out of your life:

1. Watch a funny movie.
2. Try an activity you have never done before.
3. Read a romance novel.
4. Go for a swim.
5. Write a letter to yourself.
6. Practice meditation.
7. Sing the lyrics to your favorite song.
8. Visualize your future.
9. Take a nap.
10. Say a prayer.
11. Play with your pets.
12. Cook your favorite meal.
13. Play with your children.
14. Take photos of a special moment.
15. Plant new flowers.
16. Clean out your closet.
17. Get a fresh haircut.
18. Go to a restaurant alone.
19. Jump on a trampoline.
20. Lie on the grass.

Creating Your Self-Care Routine

Self-care is about adopting everyday habits that promote and maintain your health and well-being. It involves listening to your body, understanding what it needs, and challenging behaviors and thoughts that bring you out of alignment in your life. Understanding the need for self-care and practicing it are two different things. Putting self-care to practice requires you to be intentional about your choices and consciously seek to align your mind, body, and spirit.

In order for a behavior to be a form of self-care it has to offer you some type of gratification. This means that not every "good behavior" is necessarily a form of self-care for you. For instance, even though meditation is good, if you don't like meditation you cannot consider it to be a form of self-care. Thus, your self-care routine consists of all the activities you find satisfying on a mental, physical, or emotional level. One person's self-care routine may look completely different from the next person's, and this is because both people may enjoy partaking in different things. This is why it's crucial to create your own self-care routine informed by the behaviors and activities you consider a form of self-care.

Follow these three steps to create your self-care routine:

Step 1: Think of What Makes You Feel Centered

Think of the various activities that make you feel whole or centered. What activities make you feel rejuvenated or at peace? For some, it may be prayer or times of reflection and for others it may be cuddling with their dog. When thinking about these activities, focus on those you can practice on a regular basis.

Step 2: Find Ways of Incorporating Those Activities into Your Daily Life

Restructure your daily routine to incorporate some of the self-care activities you love. If you are usually busy during the day, find time in the mornings or evenings to practice self-care. Remember to keep your routine fresh by switching up the activities you do each day and making sure you have a new activity to look forward to.

Step 3: Set Goals for Incorporating Self-Care Activities in Your Daily Routine

Once you have practiced a few self-care activities, evaluate the ones that feel good and have a positive impact on your mood and overall well-being. Next, create smart goals for how often you intend on practicing these activities and until when. For example, if you are planning to reduce the time spent on social media, you could make a goal to log out of your social media accounts after a certain time every day for one month. Once you have achieved this goal, you can extend the period of time to two or three months.

If you find yourself struggling to adopt a self-care routine, it may be useful to investigate where the resistance is coming from. Some people can figure out the cause of resistance from journaling and reading the letters they write to themselves, while others get to the root of the issue by visiting a professional therapist.

Why You Should Prioritize Yourself

Many of us are taught from a young age that prioritizing ourselves is a form of selfishness. The true goal, many would argue, is to be selfless and generously give all that we have to others. However, many people have taken selflessness to the extreme, pushing the limits to what they can give to others and hurting themselves in the process. Nowadays, being selfless has the negative connotation of neglecting our own needs so we can please others and fulfill their desires.

Before we can take care of anyone else, we need to take care of ourselves. It's difficult to help other people when we're not getting the help we need. Showing people love requires us to know what love feels like from personally experiencing and cultivating it. If we don't have love within us, how can we show love to others? Therefore, part of having fulfilling relationships and progressing in various aspects of our lives requires us to prioritize our well-being. Below are a few reasons to put ourselves first:

1. When We Feel Depleted, We Have Nothing to Give

When we are overwhelmed by the stresses of life and the heavy burden of responsibility on our shoulders, extending ourselves to others becomes difficult. Similarly, when we have depleted all of our energy caring for other people, we can be left feeling empty and unsatisfied with our lives. The best kind of giving anyone can do is giving from a place of abundance. If someone has an abundance of love, they can share this love with others, without it depleting. Think for a moment about the emotions, talents, and resources you have in abundance and find ways of offering those to people around you instead of the emotions, talents, and resources you lack.

2. Doing What We Love Energizes Us

When we are preoccupied with activities and tasks that we love, we cultivate a natural energy that can easily be transferred to those around us. The glow in our face makes others feel happy and we have a lot more positivity to offer. Think of a few tasks you love to do and invite your friends or family members to join you in performing them. If you are passionate about cycling, you can ask a friend to join you on a Saturday morning for a ride around the neighborhood.

3. We Can Lose Touch With Ourselves Serving Others

It's easy for us to neglect our needs when serving others. Parents who go above and beyond for their children may disconnect from their own personal goals and live to serve the needs of their children. This also appears in romantic relationships when couples disconnect to their individual hobbies and interests because they are so wrapped up in caring for each other. Losing touch with ourselves while serving others may cause us to disconnect with our personal ambitions, dreams, and interests, which leaves a gaping hole within us that nothing can fill.

4. Our Stress Can Hurt Us and Those Around Us

When we don't check-in with how we are feeling, we can project negative emotions and create stress for us and those around us. Carrying more responsibility at work can lead to a cycle of stress, which ends up feeling like the norm. This surmounting stress can lead to mental health illnesses, like depression or anxiety, and also cause conflict among colleagues.

5. We Can Compromise Our Performance

When you haven't had enough hours of sleep at night, how do you generally feel the next morning? Many people will feel tired, grumpy, and unable to concentrate. When we neglect to prioritize our own well-being, like getting sufficient rest, we can indirectly compromise our performance and productivity at work and throughout the day. We become friendlier, high-performing people at work when we are well rested, eat a healthy breakfast, and feel mentally strong.

Chapter 7: Evolving as a Single Unit and as a Whole

The late John Bradshaw once said, "The spiritual quest is not some added benefit to our life, something you embark on if you have the time and inclination. We are spiritual beings on an earthly journey. Our spirituality makes up our beingness." (Wilner, 2014) When we speak about self-care, it's imperative that we include spiritual growth. Dedicating time to learn about our spirituality is as important as learning about our identity. Spirituality is a broad term that can mean a lot of things for a lot of different people, however, at its simplest form spirituality is a deep connectedness and openness to God. By growing in your spirituality, you become reliant on your Higher Power to help you cope with obstacles in life and experience a sense of inner peace even amidst external crises. Below are five additional benefits of prioritizing your spiritual growth:

1. We Feel a Sense of Hopefulness

Spirituality gives us a sense of hopefulness, especially during difficult times. Because we are deeply connected to God, we know there is always help, goodness, and healing available to us whenever we desire it. Spirituality makes us optimistic about the future and allows us to believe our goals are truly possible.

2. We Gain Compassion and Understanding

When we begin to grow spiritually, we are more understanding of others and feel compassionate toward others' misfortunes. Instead of being judgmental about someone's life choices, we are willing to learn about their way of life and find commonalities. Growing in compassion also helps us build and maintain healthy relationships with others, learning how to forgive one another quickly and return to a place of peace.

3. We Gain a Sense of Purpose

Spirituality gives us a greater sense of purpose and makes us feel like we are alive to do something magnificent with our lives. We feel compelled to make a contribution to our families, communities, and workplaces because of the confidence we have in who we are. Without spirituality, we can live without a clear direction about where we are going or find it difficult to see the meaning behind what we do.

4. We are Inspired

Spirituality inspires us to break free from conventional wisdom and envision the kind of life we want. Spirituality makes the impossible possible and because of this, we have a greater appreciation for life. All it takes is to look at the infinite beauty all around us and see how fortunate we are to create our own beautiful lives.

5. We Have Peace of Mind

The greater part of spirituality is connecting to a Higher Power that is the source of all things good. In some religions, this Higher Power is a deity or god and in others the Higher Power is simply energy. Knowing there is a Higher Power gives us peace of mind, especially when we feel lost or afraid, because we understand there is something greater than ourselves out there and we are never alone.

7 Stages of Spiritual Growth

You are a spiritual being and have the potential to embrace your spirituality. Many people embark on personal development journeys or healing journeys. Similarly, spiritual journeys exist. Embarking on a spiritual journey is a choice. You decide how far along the spiritual path you desire to go and how much spirituality you embrace in your life. Below are the seven stages of spiritual growth you can look forward to:

Stage 1: Innocence

When you are born, you come forth into the world in a state of innocence. Your early childhood years are simple and as long as you are healthy and have a good home environment, you live in a peaceful world. As a baby, you still have a strong connection to the Divine from which your consciousness has just emerged. As you grow up and are taught to follow societal norms, you lose touch with your spiritual being and immerse yourself fully in the human experience.

Stage 2: Fear and Ego

As you grow older, your ego emerges and you realize how dependent you are on other people. The pure, unfiltered love you showed in your early years is slowly replaced with suspicion and fear. You see that your survival is tied to other people, and you learn how to please and manipulate them. Moreover, you create your personality and all of the stories that will shape and define who you are.

Stage 3: Power

Later on in life, you find the only way to overcome fear is by earning power. This causes you to seek success in your career, health, and relationships. The greater your level of stability in all areas of your life, the less fearful life becomes. Being healthy, having a good job, and raising a family provides you with a lot more control and a sense of security.

At stage three, many people are faced with a choice; they can either continue seeking materialistic pleasures for a stronger sense of security or they can continue seeking a deeper meaning to life and proceed to stage four.

Stage 4: Giving

Those who reach stage four realize there is more to life than accumulating materialistic possessions and increasing personal power. Instead of making your life center around you, you put the focus on other people and your community at large. This doesn't mean stop prioritizing yourself or your spiritual growth, but that you are more comfortable with giving and receiving. It's important to note that giving can still be ego-driven since it does give you a sense of power over others. For instance, you give because it makes you look responsible and generous.

Giving from the perspective of the ego will always make you expect to receive something in return for your giving. Even though this type of giving has merit, it can hinder you from growing spiritually, keeping you trapped under the leadership of your ego. Those who proceed to stage five learn how to give from a place of love and compassion, not looking to be rewarded for their generosity.

Stage 5: Seeking

Many people begin or start taking their spiritual practices seriously at stage five. They develop a deep longing for enlightenment and learning about spiritual truths. Instead of living aimlessly, they search for meaning in everything they do and make decisions by first connecting to their hearts. At this stage, many people may also start thinking about their purpose, asking themselves questions like "Why am I here?"

Stage 6: Wisdom

After a period of seeking, your mind fully awakens and you gain a deeper level of self-awareness. You can make sense of the past and why everything had to occur the way it did and this gives you a source of strength to face present and future challenges. You become aware of your actions and behaviors and can trace each one to a feeling or a thought that you've had. Change becomes possible at this stage because you are less likely to hide any troublesome behavior from yourself. For instance, if you notice a bad habit, you can begin the process of replacing it with a good one, without trying to talk yourself out of it.

While the reawakening of your mind can be an empowering moment, it's important not to feel like you are special or positioned high above anyone else for being able to tap into new depths of wisdom and truth. At stage six you have overcome a good portion of your ego, but not all. Avoid thinking highly of yourself or believing you have reached the pinnacle of your spirituality. Recognize the ego, but refuse to be distracted by it. Continue your spiritual walk with humility and devotion.

Stage 7: Spirit

In the previous stage, your mind fully awakened but in the final stage, your heart fully awakens. You experience a stronger and deeper connection with the Divine or God and for the first time, feel united with God in your spirit. There is no longer any barrier or separation between you and God because you have merged and become one. You may still live in the world but you are able to transcend the worldly experience and tap into an eternal experience of love, peace, and joy.

Once you reach the seventh stage, you will realize there is no longer a need to make choices. Since you are one with God, you believe in your heart you are well taken care of and all of your needs are met. Even when you set daily intentions or create long-term goals, you are not tied to the outcome because you trust the best possible results to happen for you.

4 Strategies to Strengthen Your Spirituality

Your spiritual journey will continue to develop as you grow and outgrow certain phases in your life. There will be times where you are too preoccupied with the cares of life to give your spirituality any attention and other times where you don't seem to care about the materialistic pursuits and only desire to connect deeper to your spiritual self. Moreover, the truths and spiritual practices that worked for you in the beginning of your spiritual journey may not work for you as you develop spiritually, and you will need to seek higher truths and alternative spiritual practices.

Strengthening your spirituality is a process that requires your full participation. You cannot expect to develop spiritual strength without doing any kind of spiritual training. Many spiritual leaders and teachers throughout history had to endure excruciating pain and sacrifices to prove their dedication to what they believed to be true. Likewise, you will need to commit to your spiritual journey and dedicate yourself to spiritual principles and beliefs so you can continue to grow spiritually. Here are four strategies to strengthen your spirituality:

1. Practice Forgiveness

You have probably been hurt countless times and hurt others countless times too. It's human nature to make mistakes or do corrupt deeds. Holding a grudge hardens your heart and causes negativity to fester within you. After some time, you become mentally, emotionally, and physically sick from the build up of negativity you have been withholding. Forgiving others who have wronged you isn't an easy decision, but it can strengthen your spirituality and lead you toward the path of wholeness.

2. Be Open and Honest With Others

One of the focuses of spirituality is forming deeper connections with other people, animals, and nature.

Ultimately, all of creation is one and every living species is connected in some way. In your personal relationships, learn how to be authentic in expressing who you are and what you desire. It can be very tempting to operate from your "false self," which is the personality you create so others may approve of you. But true power and love is transferred from one person to another when we choose to be vulnerable and reveal our shortcomings, fears, and uncertainties to each other. Together, we realize no one is perfect.

3. Explore Your Inner Self

Getting to know who you are can help you strengthen your spirituality. The world can so often discourage us from listening to our own heart's desires or forming our own opinions about matters. This causes us to separate from true self and adopt a false self. By spending time getting to know who we are, we will easily pick up when our mood is low or when we feel depleted. With the knowledge of who we are, we can create a life full of meaning for ourselves and live an authentic life. Some of the exercises to explore the inner self include:

- Journaling and tracking patterns in thoughts and behaviors
- Adopting a spiritual practice that grounds you and makes you feel whole
- Learning how to express your truth, without watering it down for others
- Spending time alone doing an activity you are passionate about

- Listening to calming music or playing a musical instrument
- Painting what you are feeling at the moment

Keeping in Touch With Family Will Keep You Feeling Whole

It's common for family tension to pull families apart, or for a family to lose connection when it is large. The well-being of the family unit impacts an individual's well-being because of the strong bonds that are forged within families. When a family is going through a hard time, it's common for the individuals within the unit to experience difficulties as well.

The secret ingredient to strengthening families and making sure each individual feels accepted is communication. Communication is what makes families feel connected, even when they haven't seen each other in a while. This feeling of connectedness contributes to everyone's happiness and reinforces the sense of belonging they feel within the family.

Communicating openly in a family isn't easy, especially when it isn't the norm. The best way to create a culture of open and honest communication is to start showing as much support as you can. Your family members are a strong pillar of support during challenging times in your life. When communication is poor or compromised, it may not feel safe to confide in them about what you are going through. Show support to receive support in return. Create a new culture in your household of showing up for each other and allowing every member of the family (both young and old) to freely voice how they feel without being judged. The more support someone feels, the safer it feels to communicate.

Below are a few types of support you can offer to your family members:

- **Emotional support:** Making your relatives feel better when they are in a poor mood and sharing happy memories or moments together.
- **Esteem support:** Making your relatives feel comfortable in their own abilities and skills and acknowledging them when they have done something commendable.
- **Network support:** Paying attention to all of your close relatives, both young and old, and making them feel like they are a valuable member of the family.
- **Tangible support:** Offering financial support or cooking meals for sick members of the family. Making efforts to unburden them when they need help.
- **Informational support:** Sharing family values and beliefs with relatives so they are informed about how the family operates and what is expected of them.

Once you have instilled a culture of support, it's important to keep those lines of communication open. Communication looks different for every family. Some families are open in sharing all sorts of information with each other, across generations, while other families are only comfortable expressing certain types of information across generations. Learn how open your family is in sharing information with one another. Do you have a family group chat on Whatsapp? Does your family host conference calls on Zoom? Do you have traditions where you meet up at specific people's homes for a family lunch?

If you know that all of your siblings have Whatsapp for example, you can create a sibling group and start chats related to topics or situations you are all experiencing. If you haven't reached out to a family member, find out what channel they prefer using. If they don't have social media, send them an email, text message, or make a phone call. Reaching out in an unconventional way is better than not reaching out at all.

Teach yourself to make contact with family members whenever you think about them. You might say, "Why should I always be the one reaching out first?" The answer is simple: when you reach out to someone you miss, how does that make you feel? You probably have a rush of positive emotions flowing within you, which make you feel better about yourself. The positive emotions you get when you contact someone you miss is the reward you earn for making the first move and calling a relative first. If you don't take the risk and reach out to your relatives, no communication will be made and this may strain your relationships.

Strengthening the relationship with your family also requires you to be a good listener. When you listen without formulating a counter-argument in your head, you can appreciate what the speaker is saying. You don't have to agree with everything your relatives say or do, but it's important to give them the space to voice how they feel without feeling ashamed. When you listen, you are acknowledging the speaker's experience and showing them how much you respect them as a person. This makes it easier for them to open up to you again in the future, since they feel understood and respected by you. Listening becomes a powerful skill when speaking to younger or older members of your family. You may not understand the experience your child is going through, but because you have listened to them explain it, they feel accepted and acknowledged.

When you don't understand a relative's sudden behavioral changes or decision-making skills, it's better to ask them for an explanation than to make an assumption. Be curious about the way others think and make decisions. Even if you disagree with the choices they have made, ask for clarity and at least try to understand where they might be coming from.

Strengthening the Relationship With Your Partner

Every couple desires a healthy relationship; one where they feel comfortable expressing themselves and feel heard by their partner. These types of healthy relationships don't happen magically, though. Strong relationships require both parties to put in the work in strengthening the union. There are four healthy habits that couples practice to keep their union strong:

1. They Aren't Afraid to be Vulnerable

Vulnerability is a superpower in relationships that creates an environment of intimacy. When couples feel safe to speak their mind or express how they feel to one another, they are able to connect on a deeper emotional level. Even when conflict arises in their relationship, the strong connection between them keeps them drawn to each other. Vulnerability also offers couples the opportunity to know each other's true selves. They get to look beyond their partner's public persona and spend time learning about who they really are.

2. They Are Compassionate

Couples in strong relationships tend to be kind toward each other. One is able to put themselves in the other's shoes and sympathize with what they are going through. Even during times of conflict, compassionate couples are able to work together to resolve the issue so they can restore the peace in their relationship. Compassionate couples are also less prone to judge or criticize their partner for their noticeable flaws. They recognize their partner is just as flawed as they are and thus, they are accepting of each other's differences.

3. They Are Spontaneous

It's difficult for many couples to keep the initial spark or attraction that made them fall in love with each other. This is true especially in long-term relationships where couples live together and probably have children or family to prioritize. Reigniting the spark requires consistent effort, like being spontaneous and trying something different every now and again. Each couple may define spontaneity differently. It's all about doing something that's not part of the ordinary routine.

4. They Settle Arguments Quickly

When an argument is kept going for too long, it can snowball and turn into a bigger and uglier outcome. For instance, a small dispute about dirty dishes that's kept going for too long and turns into a full-on argument that has nothing to do with the initial dispute. Couples in strong relationships prioritize reaching a resolution than trying to win the argument. Even though they may be frustrated, they are able to communicate effectively and ask open-ended questions to understand each other's experiences.

These four habits can strengthen your relationship, but they don't make your relationship. There isn't a mathematical formula or "secret ingredient" to a long-lasting and strong relationship. It's all the little things you do consistently that add up to showing you care about preserving your partnership. Below are small, but powerful, things you can do everyday to make your relationship stronger:

- **Ask your partner something new.** Instead of repeatedly asking your partner how they day went, ask them about a challenging part of their day or the highlight of their day. New types of questions can foster meaningful discussions that continue for many hours and provide both of you with value.
- **Plan a date night.** Busy schedules shouldn't stop you and your partner from having quality time together. Scheduling date nights can give you something to look forward to and can keep the intimacy flowing in your relationship.
- **Express your appreciation.** When your partner's kindness or generosity has become normal everyday behavior, it is easy to take it for granted. When you come home to a delicious home-cooked meal, remember how much time and effort it took for your partner to prepare the meal. Expressing your appreciation, even with a simple "Thank you" can make your partner feel acknowledged for their contribution.
- **Remember the small things.** When your partner shares something with you, remember to follow up the following day or week and ask them for feedback. If your partner shares their preference, make a mental note and make sure you take it into consideration when relevant.
- **Show your affection.** Showing affection toward your partner can communicate how much you care about them. Every couple has their own way of showing affection. It's always

advised to ask your partner how they would like affection shown to them, and vice versa.

Toxic People: How to Spot Them and Their Toxic Behaviors

We have all had at least one encounter with a toxic individual in our lives. At first, we may not have recognized their toxic behaviors but after some time, we felt drained or miserable whenever we were around them. Toxic people are good takers but not good givers. They are naturally drawn to givers because they cannot provide themselves with their own needs. The danger of toxic people lies in their subtlety and how they disguise their toxic behavior as being someone else's fault.

If you find yourself always questioning someone's toxic behavior but for some reason see it as being a misunderstanding of their behaviors, you have probably fallen into the trap laid out by the toxic individual. Identifying toxic behaviors is the first step in freeing yourself from falling under the influence of toxic people. Here are a few ways you can spot a toxic person:

1. They Switch Between Different Personas

Toxic people are never straightforward about who they are. (perhaps if they were, you would see their toxic nature in plain sight) They will keep you guessing about their personality, switching from being sweet and pleasant on one day to mysterious and irritable the next. Usually, you will wonder what you have done to upset the individual or how their attitude has changed so drastically. The truth is, there probably isn't anything wrong, but they will never put your mind at peace about it.

What to do: When a toxic person switches between different personas, give them space to work through their emotions without getting involved in their emotional storm. Let them know you are available to listen when they are ready to talk about it. If the issue is too complicated, the best person to talk to would be a professional counsellor.

2. They Are Very Manipulative

If you feel as though you are the only person carrying the relationship or offering support, it's probably because you are. Healthy relationships are supposed to be reciprocal; achieving the perfect balance between give and take. A toxic person may make you feel like you owe them something for their generosity. They are constantly keeping score of what they do for you so they can ask for favors later on.

What to do: You don't need to feel guilty for accepting someone's gift or acts of service if you are equally as giving. However, avoid gifts that don't feel like gifts. If you don't trust the person's intentions for doing something good for you, ask them to openly tell you why they have done it and what they expect in return for it.

3. They Won't Own Their Feelings

Instead of owning their feelings, toxic people will make others responsible for how they feel. For instance, if they are feeling upset, they will blame their friend or partner for bringing about this strong emotion. This is known as projection; a way of dumping one's feelings and thoughts on someone else. If you find yourself trying to justify why you didn't mean to make the toxic person feel bad, chances are they have already convinced you that you are responsible for how they feel.

What to do: You are not responsible for how someone else feels since they are in control of what they choose to feel in any given moment. If someone chooses to respond in anger, that choice is their responsibility. Be clear on what your intentions are in engaging with the toxic person in a conversation and refuse to accept responsibility that isn't yours to assume.

Many toxic people are unaware of their behaviors or how their behaviors affect those around them. Nevertheless, those who intentionally seek to hurt you are not worth your time and investment into the relationship. You might think a toxic person's behavior won't affect you, but after some time, their behaviors start to cause unnecessary stress and drama in your life. We often hear people say you are the product of the five people you spend most of your time with. If you are spending a lot of time with a toxic person, you will eventually compromise your own mental health. The best solution is to distance yourself from these people as soon as you identify their toxic ways. Below are five people you need to avoid at all cost.

1. The Gossiper

Gossipers enjoy speaking about other people instead of speaking about what's occurring in their own lives. Gossip is usually nasty because it focuses on the negative circumstances or misfortune others are experiencing. It is never uplifting or positive in nature and this is why it becomes toxic.

2. The Overly-Sensitive Person

There are some people who don't seem to have any control over their emotions. This makes them easily offended by even the smallest of remarks. Overly-sensitive people switch moods quickly, making it difficult to sustain a conversation with them or get them to understand your experience without stepping on their toes.

3. The Victim

Victims seek protection and empathy from others to the point of draining other people's energy. A victim always has a crisis happening in their life which they need others to fix. Even when you provide a victim with a solution, they are unable to follow through and assume responsibility for their own life.

4. The Narcissist

The narcissist is unable to give in a relationship because they expect others to do all of the giving on their behalf. They are self-absorbed and only see people as tools to boost their self-esteem or help them achieve certain ends. People in relationships with narcissists will often feel alone even though their friend or partner is right there. This is because the narcissist has emotionally checked out of the relationship and finds no real value to add.

5. The Envious

Envious people believe that the next person's life is much better than theirs. Even when something good happens in an envious person's life, they tend to compare it to someone else's fortune or success. Envious people will downplay your accomplishments and make you feel as though you are equally as stuck as they feel.

Once you have identified these people at work or in your friendship group, remove yourself from their environment. For instance, if they like to hang out in the cafeteria during lunch breaks, avoid sitting in the cafeteria. Find yourself a new spot. If you cannot distance yourself from them physically, you will need to distance yourself emotionally. Avoid trying to fix their problems or entering their emotional chaos. If you need to engage with them, do so in a rational manner and end the conversation once the main points have been discussed. When you notice a toxic person trying to push your buttons, understand the trick they are playing and disengage from the conversation. It won't help trying to debate or argue with a toxic person because their behavior is too irrational.

Conclusion

No one is born knowing how to behave correctly or understand the kind of habits necessary for a productive and successful life. Many times, we need to fall first and go through obstacles before we can consider making lifestyle adjustments and living a healthier, more liberating life.

Think back to when you learned how to ride a bicycle for the first time. Were you able to get on the bicycle and start paddling with ease? Of course not. You probably fell a few times, sat on the grass and encouraged yourself to keep going, until eventually riding a bicycle came naturally. Life is a lot like learning how to ride a bicycle. It takes many years of going off track and picking yourself up again to live a meaningful life. I wish the process was a much smoother ride, but many times we come out on the other side with victory scars.

I remember when I realized the only constant in life was change. The thought of having to be comfortable with change made me uncomfortable! I mean, who desires to adjust their behaviors and lifestyles every few years or take on more responsibility? Even though I wasn't ready for change, I knew change would come anyways. Instead of fighting against the inevitable, it felt easier to shift my mindset and learn positive habits that would make accepting change less of a struggle

The positive habits I adopted improved the quality of my life and for the first time, I felt in control of my words and actions. I could decide how I felt about a situation and the decisions I would make to bring positive solutions in a difficult situation. It was empowering to know I could direct my life in whatever direction I chose to take it.

The good news is that change is possible for anyone who desires it with a willing heart. Changing your behaviors and adopting new ones isn't an easy process, since your mind has already created a standard or acceptable norm. Just like anything in life, though, you can make progress with enough practice.

When people seek health and change, they are led by a strong desire. Perhaps they want to progress in their career, nurture their relationships, or prioritize their mental and spiritual well-being. This strong desire or goal sets the precedent for the kind of life they are hoping for. It also creates new expectations on the kind of lifestyle they ought to live. Someone who desires to improve their health may need to switch to a healthy diet and incorporate physical exercise into their daily routine. Incorporating these smaller activities into their daily routine will help them achieve their ultimate health goal.

If we were to summarize what it takes to master any particular habit, it would be dedication. To master a habit, you need to shift your mindset and adopt positive beliefs which will encourage you to keep going during tough times. No longer can you allow negative thoughts to sit in your mind and influence your outlook on life. Remember that your brain naturally finds it easier to think of the worst case scenarios than it does dwelling on positive thoughts. Therefore, make it a point to correct negative thoughts and reinforce a new norm in the way you think.

You would also need to organize your day better, making sure that from the time you wake up to the time you go to bed, you are making good use of your time and remaining focused on your goals. The one thing you have in common with a billionaire is that both of you have 24 hours in a day. Assess how you are spending your 24 hours and whether you are making time to focus on your daily tasks, like going to work, and your goals which will ultimately draw you closer to your dreams. Be intentional with every task you choose to prioritize each day. Ask yourself whether the task is positive and can benefit you or your future in any way. Mindless distractions like sitting on the couch and watching TV for hours or scrolling through your social media and stalking your favorite celebrities, aren't considered intentional activities. These activities will steal a lot of your time and cause unnecessary delays in your progress.

Mastering a habit may sound like a time-consuming skill to acquire. This is because you cannot master a habit without making several adjustments to how you live. When your positive habits are practiced regularly, though, your brain will learn the pattern and start performing them automatically. Soon enough, you will be performing positive habits without even realizing it.

What does this mean for you? It means the hardest part in your journey of self-improvement and seeking the life of your dreams is the beginning phase. You'll have to choose to leave certain bad habits behind and embrace new ones. Your dedication and focus at the beginning of your journey will help you make the necessary changes to position you for success in life.

All that's left for you to do now is implement the strategies and tips offered to you in this book. The sooner you can begin your new practices, the sooner they will become new behaviors in your life. Feel free to refer to this book whenever you need inspiration for good habits to adopt in your career, relationships, health, and spirituality.

If you have found this book valuable, please may you leave a review. Your support is deeply appreciated.

References

20 Tips for maintaining a healthy work-life balance. (n.d.). Www.roche.com. https://www.roche.com/careers/our-locations/asia/india/service/folder/20_tips_for_maintain.htm

AZQuotes. (2021). *Bill Gates quotes about computers.* A-Z Quotes. https://www.azquotes.com/author/5382-Bill_Gates/tag/computer

Babauta, L. (2007, May 25). *10 Benefits of rising early, and how to do it.* Zen Habits. https://zenhabits.net/10-benefits-of-rising-early-and-how-to-do-it/

Berleena. (n.d.). *How to do gratitude: The 2-min morning practice to bring you more positivity.* Berleena | Intuitive Eating Coach. Retrieved March 9, 2021, from https://www.berleena.com/blog/gratitude-2-min-practice

Blacksea, G. (2020, June 10). *How to get super clear on your priorities.* Life Goals Mag. https://lifegoalsmag.com/super-clear-priorities/

Boyes, A. (2020, February 4). *How to get more pleasure out of everyday life.* Psychology Today. https://www.psychologytoday.com/us/blog/in

-practice/202002/how-get-more-pleasure-out-
everyday-life

Bradberry, T. (2015, November 10). *10 Toxic people you should avoid at all costs*. Forbes. https://www.forbes.com/sites/travisbradberry /2015/11/10/10-toxic-people-you-should- avoid-at-all-costs/?sh=15c8f78d61db

Brewer, J. (2019, December 5). *How to break up with your bad habits*. Harvard Business Review. https://hbr.org/2019/12/how-to-break-up- with-your-bad-habits

Canfield, J. (2019, January 2). *The reason you need to practice daily affirmations*. America's Leading Authority on Creating Success and Personal Fulfillment - Jack Canfield. https://www.jackcanfield.com/blog/practice- daily-affirmations/

CDC. (2020, February 11). *National Diabetes Statistics Report, 2020*. Centers for Disease Control and Prevention. https://www.cdc.gov/diabetes/library/features /diabetes-stat- report.html#:~:text=New%20in%202020%2C %20the%20report

Cherry, K. (2020, April 29). *Why our brains are hardwired to focus on the negative*. Verywell Mind. https://www.verywellmind.com/negative-bias- 4589618

Clancy, T. (2018, March 27). *4 Daily practices to strengthen your relationship*. One Love

Foundation.
https://www.joinonelove.org/learn/4-daily-practices-to-strengthen-your-relationship/

Clifton, J. (2017, June 13). *The world's broken workplace.* Gallup. https://news.gallup.com/opinion/chairman/212045/world-broken-workplace.aspx?g_source=position1&g_medium=related&g_campaign=tiles

Danielsson, M. (2021, February 17). *These 12 habits will help you reach financial freedom.* Investopedia. https://www.investopedia.com/articles/personal-finance/112015/these-10-habits-will-help-you-reach-financial-freedom.asp

Donovan, J. (2016, April 28). *Keeping in touch with family can keep you healthy.* WebMD; WebMD. https://www.webmd.com/healthy-aging/guide/family-support#1

Dr. CCC. (2020, April 29). *Financial freedom: What does it mean to you?* Cash Cow Couple. https://www.cashcowcouple.com/what-is-financial-freedom/#:~:text=What%20is%20Financial%20Freedom%3F

Eisler, M. (2017, August 25). *4 Ways to strengthen your spirituality.* Chopra. https://chopra.com/articles/4-ways-to-strengthen-your-spirituality

Firestone, L. (2017, August 17). *The unselfish art of prioritizing yourself.* Psychology Today https://www.psychologytoday.com/za/blog/compassion-matters/201708/the-unselfish-art-prioritizing-yourself

Gabriel, R. (2018, December 6). *The 7 stages of spiritual development.* Chopra. https://chopra.com/articles/the-7-stages-of-spiritual-development

Grace. (2020, May 26). *How to stay motivated by creating a reward system.* Life Chief Nation. https://lifechiefnation.com/how-to-stay-motivated-by-creating-a-reward-system/

Gregory, A. (2020, February 28). *How to set achievable goals with backward goal setting.* The Balanced Small Business. https://www.thebalancesmb.com/how-to-set-achievable-goals-with-backward-goal-setting-2951823

Gunnars, K. (2019, December 4). *How food addiction works (and what to do about it).* Healthline; Healthline Media. https://www.healthline.com/nutrition/how-food-addiction-works

Handel, S. (2018, October 4). *Morning rituals: The power of starting your day on the right note.* The Emotion Machine. https://www.theemotionmachine.com/morning-rituals-the-power-of-starting-your-day-on-the-right-note/

Hodge, A. (2012, May 25). *Start with stillness: 5 Reasons to start a morning meditation practice.* Www.onemedical.com.

https://www.onemedical.com/blog/live-well/5-reasons-meditation#:~:text=You%20start%20working%2C%20thinking%20about

Holmes, L. (n.d.). *Food is medicine – Supercharged food.* Www.superchargedfood.com. https://www.superchargedfood.com/food-is-medicine/

Huddleston, T. (2021, January 21). *Mega Millions is up to $970 million—there's one way to up the odds of winning, according to a Harvard statistics professor.* CNBC. https://www.cnbc.com/2021/01/21/how-to-up-the-odds-of-winning-a-lottery-harvard-professor.html#:~:text=The%20lottery

Huynh, C. (2017, November 17). *10 Things you can do to improve your relationship.* The Everygirl. https://theeverygirl.com/10-things-you-can-do-to-improve-your-relationship/

Jennifer. (2019, September 19). *9 Ways to be intentional every day.* Simply + Fiercely. https://www.simplyfiercely.com/be-intentional/#1-how-to-be-intentional

Lawler, M. (2020, April 5). *How to start a self-care routine you'll follow.* EverydayHealth.com. https://www.everydayhealth.com/self-care/start-a-self-care-routine/

Lufkin, B. (2019, February 14). *Is waking up early good or bad?* Www.bbc.com. https://www.bbc.com/worklife/article/201902 13-is-waking-up-early-good-or-bad

Mayne, D. (2019, September 6). *Why it's important to be honorable and keep your word*. The Spruce. https://www.thespruce.com/honoring-your-word-4153140#:~:text=Honoring%20your%20word%20is%20more

Merriam-Webster. (2009). *Definition of success*. Merriam-Webster.com. https://www.merriam-webster.com/dictionary/success

Nemo, J. (2014, December 23). *What a NASA janitor can teach us about living a bigger life*. Bizjournals.com. https://www.bizjournals.com/bizjournals/how-to/growth-strategies/2014/12/what-a-nasa-janitor-can-teach-us.html

Newport Academy. (2019, October 7). Understanding the mind-body connection. *Newport Academy*. https://www.newportacademy.com/resources/mental-health/understanding-the-mind-body-connection/#:~:text=Physical%20health%20and%20emotional%20health

OmniOne. (2016, March 31). *How can you cope when you feel pressure to succeed? :* Omni One. https://www.omnione.com/career-resources/detail/3133/how-can-you-cope-when-you-feel-pressure-to-succeed

Pan, A., Sun, Q., Bernstein, A. M., Schulze, M. B., Manson, J. E., Willett, W. C., & Hu, F. B. (2011). Red meat consumption and risk of type 2 diabetes: 3 cohorts of US adults and an updated meta-analysis. *The American Journal of*

Clinical Nutrition, 94(4), 1088–1096. https://doi.org/10.3945/ajcn.111.018978

Radcliffe, S. (2018, October 20). *Four food choices that greatly increase your diabetes risk*. Healthline. https://www.healthline.com/health-news/food-four-food-groups-that-raise-diabetes-risk-111313#Sugar-Sweetened-Drinks

Rodale, M. (2011, December 2). *20 Simple ways to get more pleasure in your life*. Prevention. https://www.prevention.com/life/a20434649/get-more-pleasure-in-your-life/

Rose, J. (2017, November 2). *5 Ways to generate different sources of income*. Forbes. https://www.forbes.com/sites/jrose/2017/11/02/different-sources-income/?sh=405b7c9e37bb

Rose, J. (2020, November 3). *Multiple streams of income: How to earn extra money in your spare time*. Good Financial Cents®. https://www.goodfinancialcents.com/multiple-streams-of-income/

Sadlier, A. (2019, April 17). *The average American only has 43 minutes of "me time" a day*. New York Post. https://nypost.com/2019/04/17/the-average-american-only-has-43-minutes-of-me-time-a-day/

Sandhu, B. (2018, January 7). *8 Reasons to have more "me time" in 2018 for a better you*. Her World Singapore. https://www.herworld.com/life/8-reasons-have-more-me-time-better-you/

Sanfilippo, M. (2020, March 3). *How to improve your work-life balance.* Business News Daily. https://www.businessnewsdaily.com/5244-improve-work-life-balance-today.html

Schmidt, L. (2020, January 1). *Start your day with a clear intention.* Chopra. https://chopra.com/articles/start-your-day-with-a-clear-intention

Scott, E. (n.d.). *Wealth formula: The secret to wealth creation.* Www.streetdirectory.com. Retrieved March 12, 2021, from https://www.streetdirectory.com/travel_guide/143227/how_to_grow_wealth/wealth_formula_the_secret_to_wealth_creation.html

Team Tony. (2018, July 11). *How to do what you love and love what you do.* Tonyrobbins.com. https://www.tonyrobbins.com/career-business/how-to-do-what-you-love/

Vaughn, K. (2018, May 5). *You will spend 90,000 hours of your lifetime at work. Are you happy?* Medium. https://kassandravaughn.medium.com/you-will-spend-90-000-hours-of-your-lifetime-at-work-are-you-happy-5a2b5b012off

Webb, N. (2021, February 23). *The 7 stages of financial freedom.* @Spaceshipau. https://www.spaceship.com.au/learn/the-seven-stages-of-financial-freedom/

Weisenberger, J. (2017, August 4). *The power of a morning ritual.* Calorie Control Council. https://caloriecontrol.org/the-power-of-a-

morning-
ritual/#:~:text=Some%20common%20mornir_
g%20rituals%20include

Werner, M. (n.d.). Practice #2 mindful breathing
meditation. In *Smith Center*. Retrieved March
8, 2021, from https://smithcenter.org/wp-
content/uploads/files/downloads/mindful-
breathing-meditation.pdf

*Why is physical activity so important for health and
wellbeing?* (2017, January 14). Www.heart.org.
https://www.heart.org/en/healthy-
living/fitness/fitness-basics/why-is-physical-
activity-so-important-for-health-and-wellbeing

Wilner, J. (2014, November 9). *Five reasons to develop
and grow your spirituality.* Psych Central.
https://psychcentral.com/blog/best-
self/2014/11/five-reasons-to-develop-and-
grow-your-spirituality#1

Young, K. (2017, November 5). *Toxic people: 12 Things
they do and how to deal with them.*
Heysigmund.com.
https://www.heysigmund.com/toxic-people/

Book 1 of 2

THE ULTIMATE

Adults Coloring Book

Is A Stress Relieving Coloring Book,
Disegned For Adults Relaxation.
With Over 100 Flowers & Animals

Jack Daniel Raymond

THIS BOOK
BELONGS TO

____

____

____

color test page

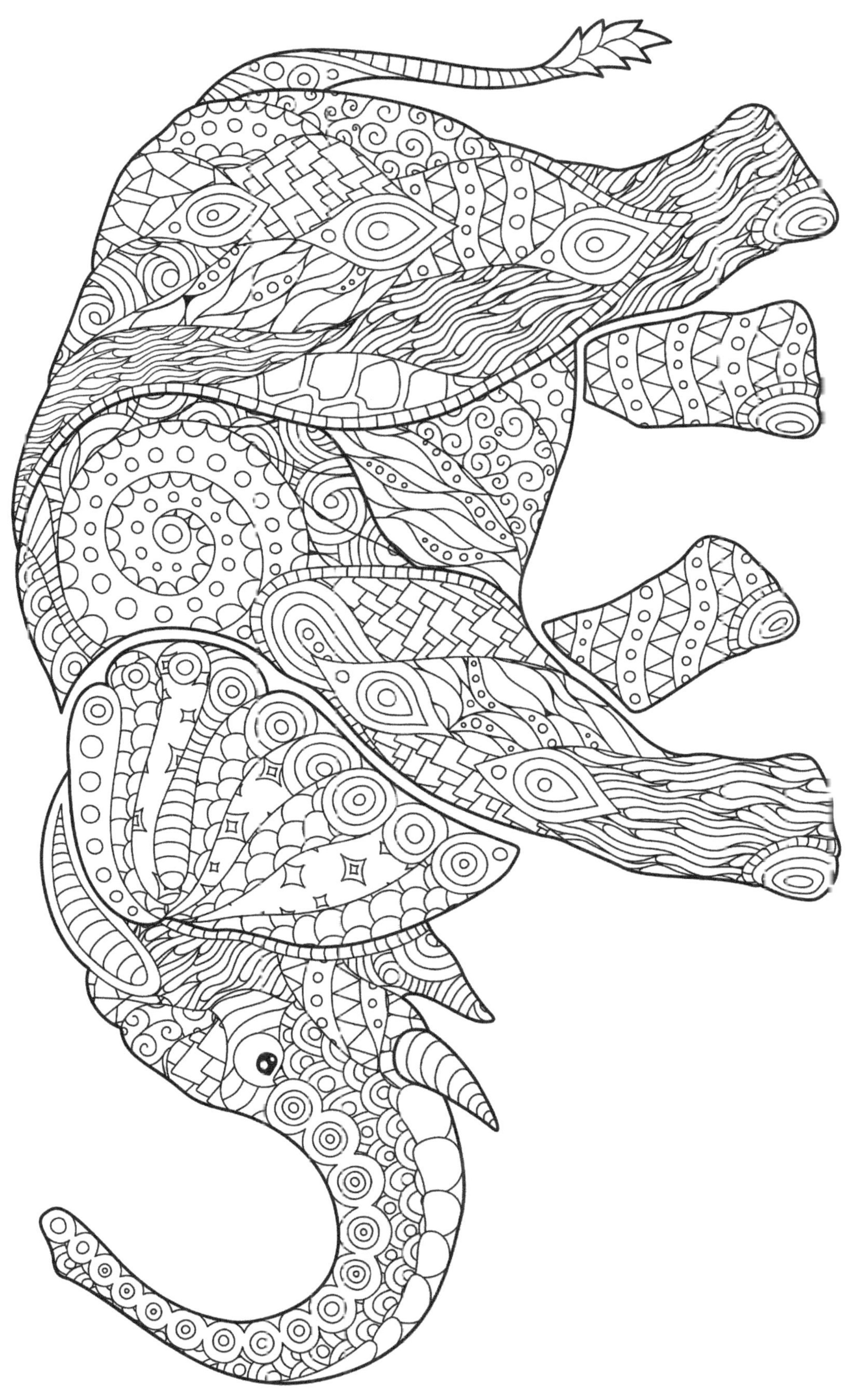

SCORPIO

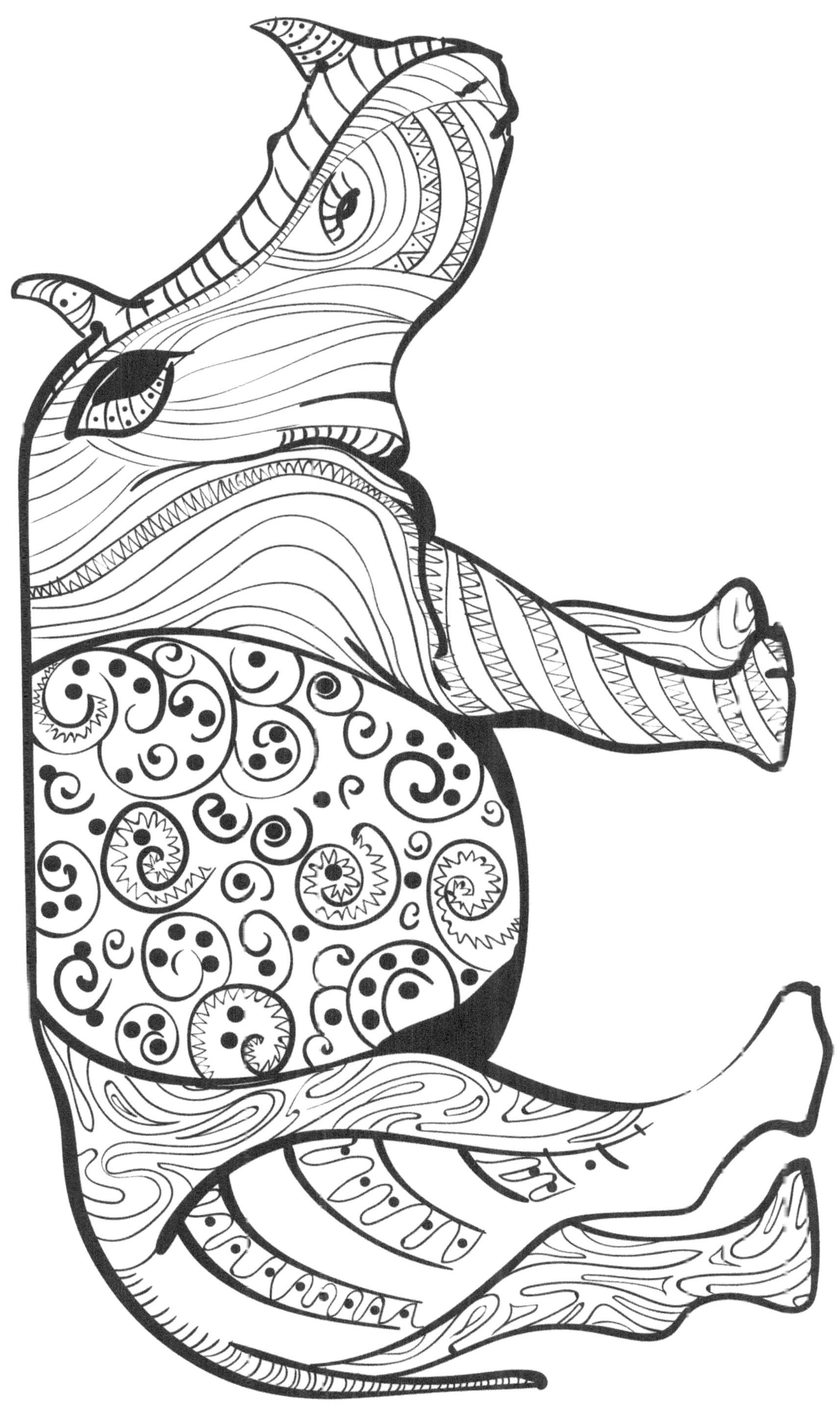

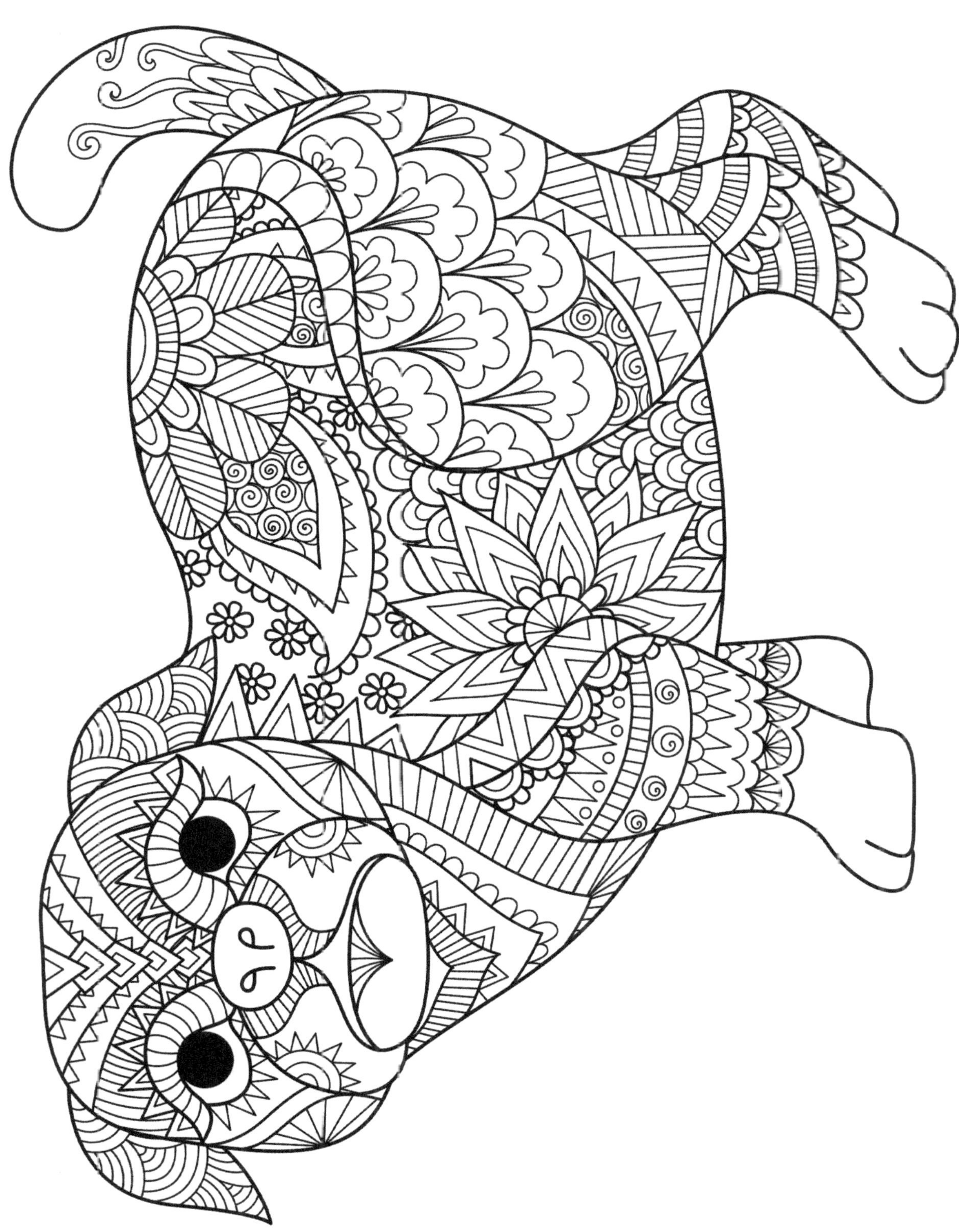

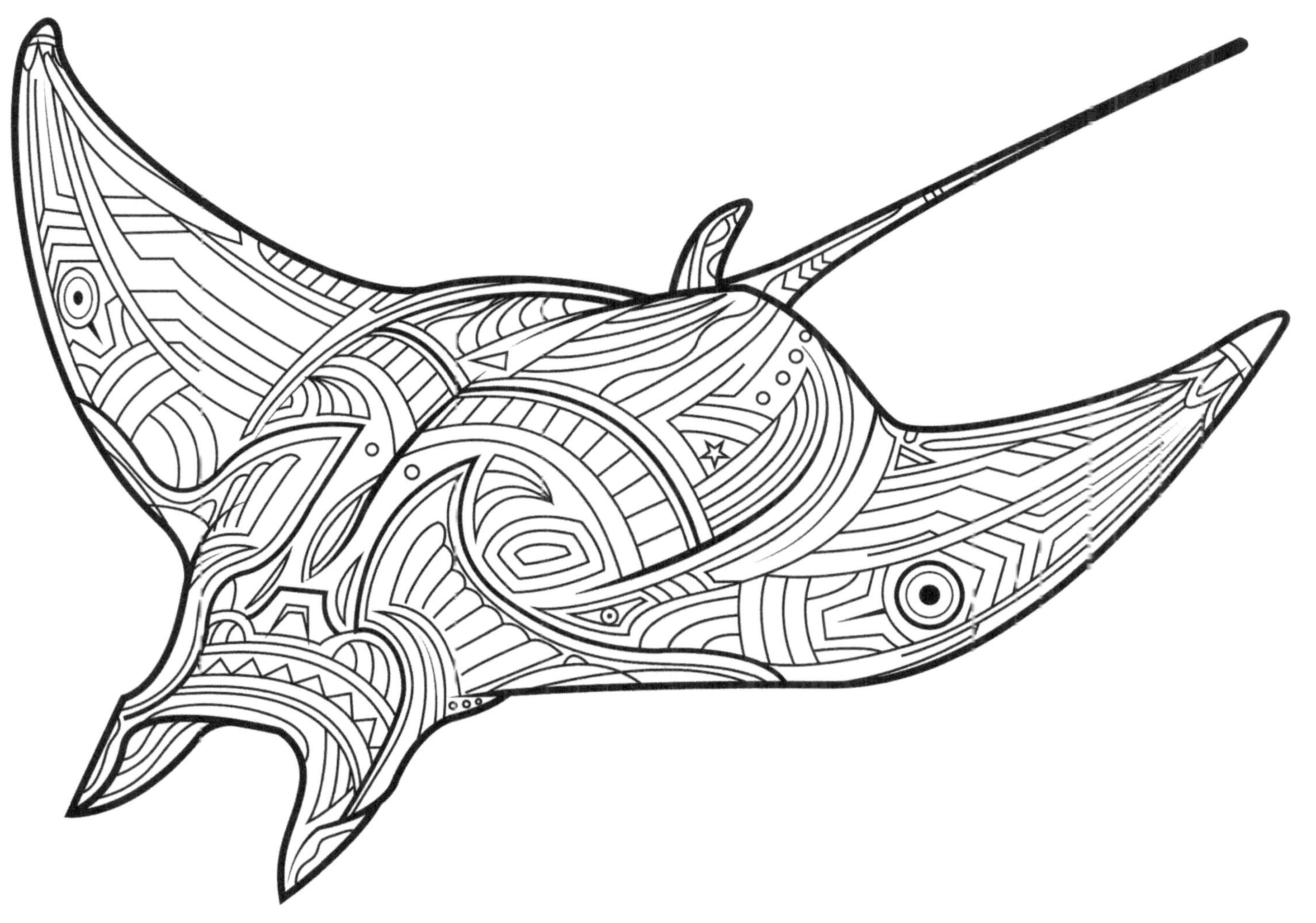

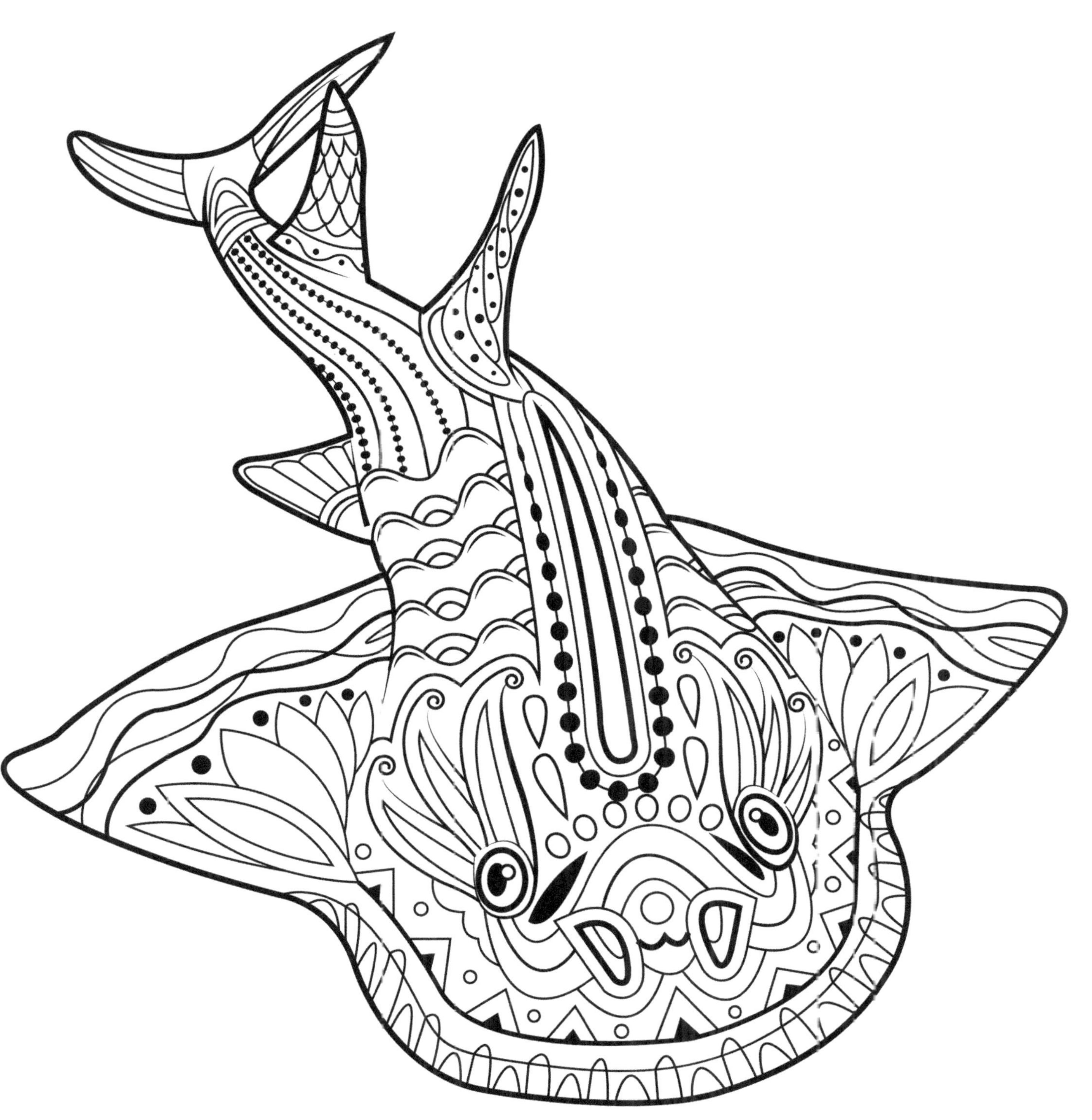

♑ CAPRICORN

CANCER

ARIES

THIS COLORING BOOK BELONGS TO

____

____

____

THIS PAGE LEFT
INTENTIONALLY BLANK

FASHION
models & designs
COLORING BOOK
FOR ADULTS
FASHION MODELS & FACES TO COLOR

THIS PAGE LEFT
INTENTIONALLY BLANK

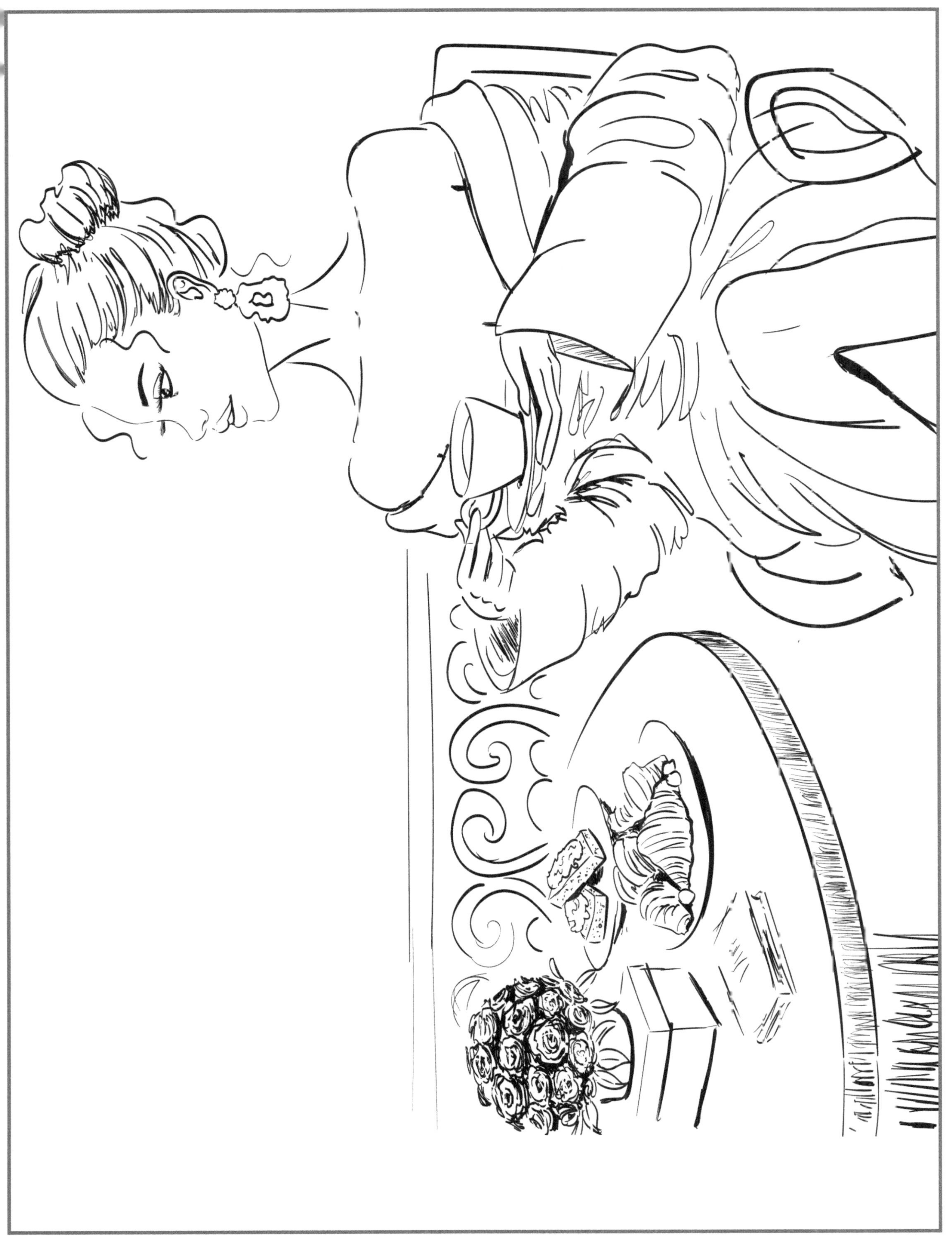

THIS PAGE LEFT
INTENTIONALLY BLANK

THIS PAGE LEFT
INTENTIONALLY BLANK

THIS PAGE LEFT
INTENTIONALLY BLANK

THIS PAGE LEFT
INTENTIONALLY BLANK

THIS PAGE LEFT
INTENTIONALLY BLANK

THIS PAGE LEFT
INTENTIONALLY BLANK

THIS PAGE LEFT
INTENTIONALLY BLANK

THIS PAGE LEFT
INTENTIONALLY BLANK

THIS PAGE LEFT
INTENTIONALLY BLANK

THIS PAGE LEFT
INTENTIONALLY BLANK

THIS PAGE LEFT
INTENTIONALLY BLANK

THIS PAGE LEFT
INTENTIONALLY BLANK

THIS PAGE LEFT
INTENTIONALLY BLANK

THIS PAGE LEFT
INTENTIONALLY BLANK

THIS PAGE LEFT
INTENTIONALLY BLANK

THIS PAGE LEFT
INTENTIONALLY BLANK

GRL
PWR

THIS PAGE LEFT
INTENTIONALLY BLANK

THIS PAGE LEFT
INTENTIONALLY BLANK

THIS PAGE LEFT
INTENTIONALLY BLANK

THIS PAGE LEFT
INTENTIONALLY BLANK

THIS PAGE LEFT
INTENTIONALLY BLANK

THIS PAGE LEFT
INTENTIONALLY BLANK

THIS PAGE LEFT
INTENTIONALLY BLANK

THIS PAGE LEFT
INTENTIONALLY BLANK

Wild Girl

THIS PAGE LEFT
INTENTIONALLY BLANK

THIS PAGE LEFT
INTENTIONALLY BLANK

THIS PAGE LEFT
INTENTIONALLY BLANK

THIS PAGE LEFT
INTENTIONALLY BLANK

THIS PAGE LEFT
INTENTIONALLY BLANK

THIS PAGE LEFT
INTENTIONALLY BLANK

THIS PAGE LEFT
INTENTIONALLY BLANK

THIS PAGE LEFT
INTENTIONALLY BLANK

THIS PAGE LEFT
INTENTIONALLY BLANK

THIS PAGE LEFT
INTENTIONALLY BLANK

THIS PAGE LEFT
INTENTIONALLY BLANK

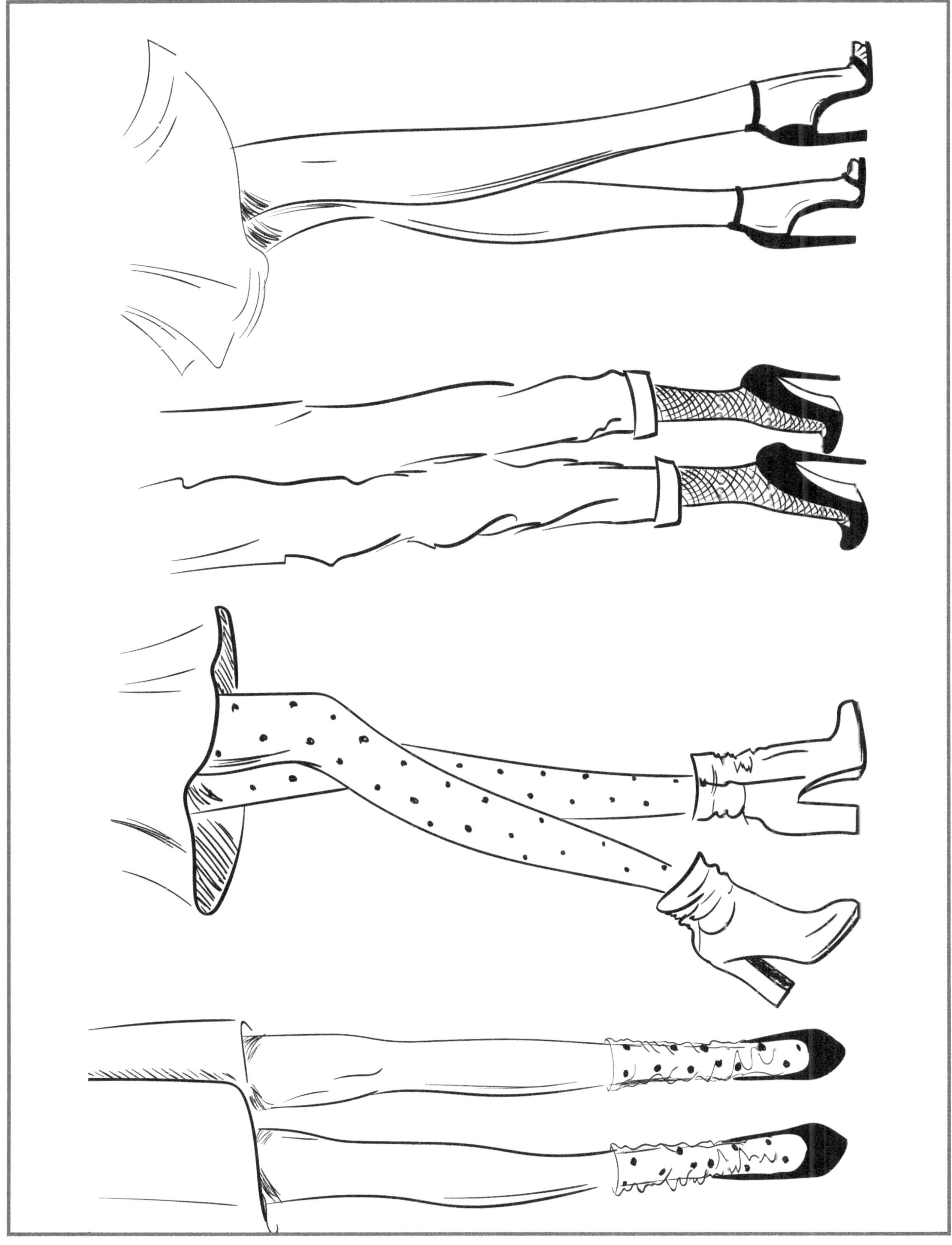

THIS PAGE LEFT
INTENTIONALLY BLANK

THIS PAGE LEFT
INTENTIONALLY BLANK

THIS PAGE LEFT
INTENTIONALLY BLANK

THIS PAGE LEFT
INTENTIONALLY BLANK

THIS PAGE LEFT
INTENTIONALLY BLANK

THIS PAGE LEFT
INTENTIONALLY BLANK

THIS PAGE LEFT
INTENTIONALLY BLANK

THIS PAGE LEFT
INTENTIONALLY BLANK

THIS PAGE LEFT
INTENTIONALLY BLANK

THYROID HEALING DIET COOKBOOK

*An **Effective Healthy** 30-day Thyroid Diet Meal Plan| Improve the condition of **Hypothyroidism, Insomnia, Thyroid Nodules & Epstein-Barr**||70 Tasty Effortless Recipes*

By Dr. Connor Anthony

Contents

THYROID HEALING DIET

Description

The Thyroid Healing Diet is a relatively new and acceptable method of managing thyroid-related disorders. While it was designed to help people with thyroid disorders eat right, its numerous health benefits are not restricted to just them. The diet contains dishes that promote both the health of the thyroid and the general wellbeing of the body.

If you are interested in a guide that will help you improve your thyroid condition and also improve your general health, then this is just the book for you.

The Thyroid Healing Diet Cookbook is a fantastic combination of a nutrition text and a recipe book. It contains information about the thyroid and the different possible disorders associated with it. It also includes a guide on the type of food that is excellent for your thyroid and the type of food that will worsen your condition.

The 70 recipes itemized in the book were carefully chosen to help you get started on your journey to eating healthy and improving your general health. The 30-day meal plan instructs you on what, when, and how much to eat. The dishes are not only pleasing to the eyes but to the stomach too.

The Thyroid Healing Diet Cookbook will teach you everything you need to know about the Thyroid diet, including;

- An introduction to the Thyroid gland
- The possible disorders and diseases affecting the Thyroid,
- The numerous health benefits,
- The principles guiding the Thyroid Healing Diet,
- A 30-day meal plan,
- 70 delicious recipes, and
- Answers to Frequently Asked Questions about Thyroid and the diet.

Introduction

Chili Pronto!

Broiled Scallops!!

Baked Coconut Shrimps!!!

These are just 3 of the 70 amazing dishes listed in the book. The dishes are all made from vegetables, that can be grown and plucked fresh from the soil, and direct animal products that have not undergone any processing.

This system of eating is not a momentary cure for your thyroid condition; it's a lifestyle. Once you develop a thyroid disorder, it becomes a lifelong condition that has to be monitored for life. The Thyroid Healing diet is designed to help you create a balance that helps you eat delicious foods without eating triggering or worsening your condition.

Everything you need to know about eating for your thyroid is mentioned in the book. Continue reading to start eating right and living well.

Chapter 1: Essentials You Need to Know About the Thyroid

The thyroid is one of the most underrated organs in the body. Most folks learned about the organ in their high school biology but forgot all about it once they successfully passed the course. When you listen to the news or come across articles containing health-related information, usually, you are educated about the dangers of ignoring your heart, lungs, or liver. Very little is mentioned about the thyroid.

More than 80% of the people diagnosed with thyroid disorders go straight to the nearest bookstore to pick up a book on it or end up *googling* and downloading e-books. Therefore, the odds that you are reading this book out of mere curiosity is very low, you are either receiving treatment or know someone who is. Whichever the reason is, you have picked up the right book. Your *hunger* for more knowledge will be satisfied, along with your stomach.

What is the Thyroid and What Does It Do?

The thyroid is a small butterfly-shaped gland positioned below the Adam's apple in the neck. It has two side lobes that are closely wrapped around the trachea and connected by a bridge called isthmus. The gland is 2 inches wide and can only be observed visibly when it is enlarged.

The thyroid is rich with blood vessels and brownish-red in color. It is part of the endocrine gland and produces hormones responsible for the regulation of various activities in the body.

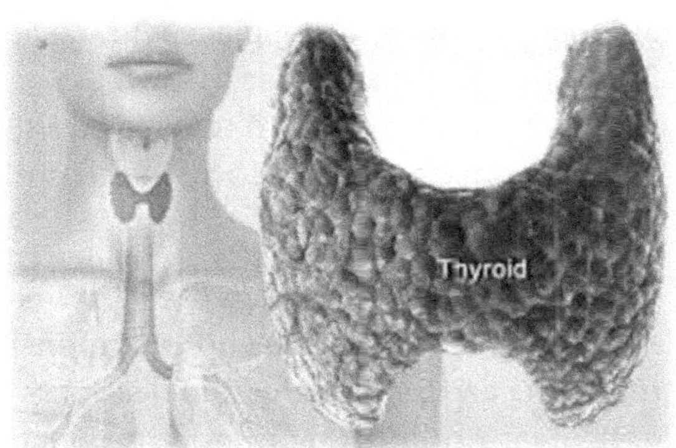

The hormones produced in the thyroid include:

- Tetraiodothyronine, popularly known as thyroxine or t4
- Triiodothyronine usually referred to as T3, and
- Calcitonin.

Together, they are collectively ca led *thyroid hormones*. Of the three hormones, Thyroxine and T3 are usually regarded as the proper thyroid hormones and are secreted in the follicular epithelial cells of the thyroid.

One of the major components necessary for the secretion of both hormones is iodine, and the concentration of iodine in the body is entirely dependent on its consumption through our diet because the element cannot be synthesized naturally in the body. During digestion, any iodine present is absorbed into the bloodstream and transported to the thyroid gland, where it used to produce hormones.

The thyroid hormones influence a variety of body functions, namely;

- Fertility
- Digestion
- Breathing
- Bodyweight
- Menstrual cycles

➢ Temperature regulation
➢ Growth and development
➢ Brain development, from infancy to childhood
➢ Heart rate, etc.

Due to the hormones it produces, the thyroid has established itself as one of the most influential organs in the body. It has a role to play in almost all the metabolic activities taking place within the body. These metabolic activities involve the chemical reactions necessary to release energy from food; the energy needed to keep the entire body running.

Thyroid disorders can range from the relatively harmless goiter (which requires no treatment) to life-threatening cancer. Usually, the disorders involve the over-production or under-production of thyroid hormones.

While most of the symptoms are typically uncomfortable, they are quite manageable when properly diagnosed and treated. Popular disorders of the thyroid gland include;

✧ Hyperthyroidism
✧ Hypothyroidism
✧ Goiter (enlarged gland)
✧ Thyroid cancer
✧ Thyroid nodules

Early Signs of Thyroid Disorders

When there is a problem with your thyroid, your body is bound to notify you. Unfortunately, these notifications are a lot similar to the notifications given by other non-thyroid related disorders. To be a hundred percent sure of the diagnosis, you have to visit your local health practitioner.

However, there is one major sign that standouts and definitely signify a problem with your thyroid. That is;

➢ Increase in size of the thyroid lobes.

Diseases Related to Thyroid

Thyroid diseases can either cause or lead to the overproduction or underproduction of thyroid hormones. Therefore, thyroid diseases are usually divided into two categories, namely;

✧ Hypothyroidism
✧ Hyperthyroidism

Hypothyroidism

Hypothyroidism is caused by the underproduction of thyroid hormones. Since the body requires a certain amount of energy to run, a reduction in the amount of energy released is bound to affect the body's regular operation.

Hypothyroidism may be caused by a number of reasons, some of them are;

➢ **Thyroiditis:** This condition results in the inflammation of the thyroid gland. The swelling may reduce the production of thyroid hormones, which subsequently leads to hypothyroidism.
➢ **Hashimoto's thyroiditis:** This is an auto-immune disorder that stops or drastically reduces the production of thyroid hormones. An auto-immune disorder occurs when the body erroneously attacks healthy indigenous cells. In this case, the cells attacked are thyroid cells. If not detected early, it could lead to the complete destruction of the thyroid organ.
➢ **Postpartum thyroiditis:** This is the swelling of the thyroid organ after childbirth. It's rare, occurring in less than 5% perinatal mothers, and disappears after about a year.
➢ **Low levels of Iodine:** Without the necessary components, such as iodine, the thyroid gland will not secrete T3 or T4 and, as a result, hypothyroidism.
➢ **Non-functioning, dead or surgical removed thyroid glands:** 1 in 4000 newborns have thyroid glands that do not function correctly. Patients of thyroid cancer, sometimes, have one or both of the lobes removed surgically to prevent the spread of the tumor. Both cases can lead to the underproduction of thyroid hormones, and thereby, hypothyroidism.

Common symptoms of hypothyroidism include;

➢ Weight gain
➢ Fatigue
➢ Dry skin
➢ Muscle aches
➢ Constipation
➢ Fluid retention
➢ Forgetfulness
➢ Poor hair texture
➢ Absentmindedness
➢ Hoarse voice
➢ Sensitivity to cold temperatures
➢ Heavy and prolonged menstrual flow
➢ Depression

Hyperthyroidism

This is caused by the overproduction of thyroid hormones. When the body produces too much thyroxine and t3, the rate of the metabolic activities performed skyrockets. Energy is produced very quickly and expended very quickly. Your body starts to run like a race car without brakes. Your heart starts to beat really fast and you are in a constant state of anxiety for no reason.

Hyperthyroidism, like other thyroid diseases, is more common to women than men and it may be caused by several factors, some of them are;

✧ Grave's disease: This condition is basically the opposite of Hashimoto's thyroiditis. It is also caused by the violent reaction of the body's immune system to an otherwise healthy indigenous cell. However, in this case, the swelling (inflammation) leads to the over-production of thyroid hormones. Several other non-thyroid related medical conditions have been known to trigger both Hashimoto and Graves disease. An example of such is the Epstein-Barr virus (EBV).

✧ Excessive Iodine: High concentrations of iodine in the bloodstream will result in the over-production of thyroid hormones. With the key component available, there will no moderation in the amount of t3 and t4 produced.

✧ Toxic Nodules: The presence of a nodule or lump on the thyroid gland will lead to the production of additional thyroid hormones. Since every action and activity in the body has a specific purpose and is regulated, the additional thyroid hormones may not necessarily be beneficial.

✧ Postpartum Thyroiditis: Perinatal mothers may suffer hyperthyroidism for a few months after childbirth. Usually, the hyperthyroidism is followed by several months of hypothyroidism. Basically, they get to experience both sides of the coin within the first year of childbirth. The condition is temporary and will resolve itself within a year.

✧ Overuse or abuse of thyroid hormones: Patients that suffer from hypothyroidism or thyroid cancer are usually prescribed thyroid hormone replacements. These replacements carry out the functions of t3, t4, and calcitonin. Abuse or unmonitored use of the drug can lead to hyperthyroidism.

✧ Thyroiditis: Like Hashimoto and Grave's disease, Thyroiditis is a double-edged sword. The inflammation can either lead to the overproduction or underproduction of thyroid hormones.

Common symptoms of hyperthyroidism include;

➢ Nervousness
➢ Increase in sweat production
➢ Insomnia
➢ Irritability
➢ Fast heart rate
➢ Increased bowel movements
➢ Absentmindedness
➢ Weight loss
➢ Enlarged thyroid gland (goiter)
➢ Muscle spasms or weakness
➢ Irregular menstrual cycles
➢ Sensitivity to heat
➢ Poor eyesight

Treatment of Hyperthyroidism and Hypothyroidism.

There are three common methods of treating Hyperthyroidism and Hypothyroidism.

— Medication
— Surgery
— Diet

❖ Medication

Thyroid replacement supplements can be prescribed to patients suffering from hypothyroidism to replace the deficient thyroid hormone in the body. While for Hyperthyroidism, medications that suppress the production of thyroid hormones are prescribed.

Sometimes, the symptoms are treated individually. Like in the case of hyperthyroidism, where drugs that regulate the heart rate are also recommended. In serious cases of hyperthyroidism, when drugs cannot completely handle the condition, radioactive ablation can be performed. This involves the injection of radioactive iodine into the body to destroy unnecessary thyroid tissue.

Note: Prescription is mentioned several times above when mentioning drugs. This is because self-medication only worsens thyroid disorder. Medical practitioners are the only individuals capable of diagnosing and prescribing drugs for the treatment of thyroid disorders.

❖ Surgery

Hypothyroidism rarely requires treatment by surgical operations. Usually, surgery is performed to remove extra tissue that causes hyperthyroidism, and biopsy is carried out on the tissue removed to determine the presence or absence of cancerous cells.

Treatment of thyroid cancer is totally different from the customary treatment of other thyroid-related disorders. It requires multiple surgeries, chemotherapy, and constant monitoring.

❖ Diet

Here, diet is mentioned as a method of treating thyroid disorders because Iodine, the major building block of thyroid hormone production, can only be obtained through food. Therefore, the type of food you eat can help you. Once diagnosed, your physician is sure to create a list of food you should eat or avoid, depending on your condition.

A good diet plan may just be all you need to resolve your disorder, however, in most cases, drugs are prescribed along with a diet change. Your physician will not go into details on the particular dishes you should eat. Rather, he will provide you with a list of foods (fruits and vegetables) you have to avoid at all costs unless you want to aggravate your condition. He may also recommend a couple of foods that should be included in your everyday diet.

Note: For specific details on dishes you are allowed to eat, you will need to contact your nutritionist. The recipes in this book were designed to cater to the needs of all individuals with thyroid disorders and only avoided foods common to all disorders. While preparing the dishes in this book, religiously compare the ingredients mentioned under each dish with your avoid-list.

Recommendations by your doctor or nutritionist come first!

Chapter 2: Thyroid Healing Diet

How does it work?

Several studies have been carried out on the effect of our eating habits on our health. Results prove that the type of food we consume into our body can either make or mar our health. Excessive consumption of fatty foods and junks can lead to heart diseases or obesity. In contrast, fruits and vegetables are known to boost the immune system.

Based on this, researchers and nutritionists all over the world are studying the components of food and what exactly makes them good for consumption. And also, how a combination of them can be used to promote health or manage diseases.

The Thyroid Healing Diet involves the consumption of foods that are known to improve the health of the thyroid. Such foods contain trace amounts of iodine, selenium, zinc, and other elements known to promote the production of thyroid hormones. When consumed in the right quantities, these foods are broken down and the necessary elements are transported via the bloodstream to the thyroid, where they assist the thyroid in performing its function.

Cautions You Need to Know When Following the Thyroid Healing Diet

It's important to note that the foods recommended under a thyroid healing diet cannot replace drugs when it comes to treating a Thyroid disorder. They only assist the drug therapy and help manage the thyroid when the drug treatment plan is completed. Do not stop taking your drugs because of the diet. This may put you in danger!

Also, it is noteworthy to mention that the foods have to be consumed in moderation because excess consumption will only have an opposite effect. The presence of a high concentration of these elements in the bloodstream will result in Hyperthyroidism.

While you are trying to manage the effects of one condition, do not create another condition!

Tips for a Successful Thyroid Healing Diet

Simply following a Thyroid healing diet may not lead to a successful management therapy. Some guidelines need to be obeyed and understood before the therapy can be effective. The most important of those guidelines include;

❖ **Avoid Heavily Processed Foods**

Recently, a lot of companies manufacturing processed foods spent tremendous amounts in marketing dollars to convince people about the "health benefits" of their products. Most of these claims are false and such products should not be considered when designing a healing diet. Try your best to use fresh vegetables and unprocessed animal products for your meals.

❖ **Use Iodized Salt**

Not all salts are healthy for Thyroid-disorder patients. The best salt recommended for thyroid patients, and almost everyone, is Iodized salt.

Note: In the places where salt is listed as part of the ingredients in this book, it's referring to *Iodized salt*.

❖ **Avoid Sugar and Fatty foods**

In general, consuming large amounts of sugars and fat is not healthy for the body. However, the craving for sugar and junks is bound to show up, especially if you are an emotional eater. The key is to find healthier substitutes for these foods. The Appetizers, Drinks, and Desserts listed in this book are healthy alternatives for processed junks.

❖ **Reduce Caffeine Intake**

Caffeine, being a powerful stimulant, is dangerous if consumed daily. While practicing healthy eating, reduce the number of caffeinated drinks you take daily.

Chapter 3: Food Guide of Thyroid Healing Diet

All the recipes of the thyroid healing diet contain ingredients that can be grown in a garden or purchased at a local grocery store. There are three categories of food when planning a Thyroid Healing Diet, these are;

- ➢ Excellent Foods
- ➢ Moderate Foods
- ➢ Worst Foods

These three categories have only one thing in common, excess consumption of any of the foods in each category is bad for your thyroid. Exercise moderation when eating.

The Best Foods for your Thyroid (Excellent and Moderate)

Excellent Foods:

These are the foods that should appear more frequently in your diets. They are proven to have good effects on the state of your thyroid. Examples of food in this category include;

- ❖ Vegetables: Seaweed, garlic, carrots, onions, zucchini, tomatoes, bell peppers, cucumbers, mushrooms, lettuce, celery, pumpkin, eggplant, etc.
- ❖ Fruits: Bananas, tangerines, oranges, apples, grapes, dates, melons, figs, coconut, lemon, lime, watermelon, blueberries, etc.
- ❖ Tubers: Irish potatoes, yams, turnips, etc.
- ❖ Legumes: Beans, peas, lentils, pulses, chickpeas, etc.
- ❖ Whole grains: Whole grain gluten-free bread, whole wheat, gluten-free pasta, buckwheat, whole oats, brown rice, barley, rye, couscous, corn, egg pasta, pita bread, etc.
- ❖ Herbs and spices: Iodized salt, thyme, cinnamon, cayenne pepper, oregano, dill, black pepper, cumin, parsley, ginger, garlic, basil, mint, nutmeg, rosemary, sage, etc.

- ❖ Greens: Beet greens, chicory, dandelion, amaranth, etc.
- ❖ Fish and seafood: Tuna, sardines, salmon, shrimps, shellfish, tilapia, clams, scallops, crabs, mussels, oysters, etc.
- ❖ Nuts and Seeds: Brazil nuts, walnuts, pumpkin seeds, hazelnuts, hemp seeds, sesame seeds, cashew nuts, sunflower seeds, macadamia nuts, etc.
- ❖ Poultry: Chicken, turkey, duck, etc.
- ❖ Poultry products: Chicken eggs, turkey eggs, quail eggs, duck eggs, etc.
- ❖ Dairy products: Yogurt, Parmesan cheese, Greek yogurt, fresh mozzarella, etc.
- ❖ Animal foods: Extra-lean ground beef, lamb, pork chops, etc.
- ❖ Healthy fats: Extra-virgin olive oil, coconut oil, etc.

Moderate Foods

These are foods that are excellent for your thyroid but should be consumed sparingly as high amounts could also be harmful to your thyroid.

- ❖ Vegetables: Cauliflower, broccoli, kale, cabbage, Brussel sprouts, spinach, beets, okra, etc.
- ❖ Fruits: Strawberries, peaches, pears, etc.
- ❖ Tubers: Sweet potatoes, cassava, etc.
- ❖ Legumes: Soybeans, soy milk, edamame beans, tofu, tempeh, etc.
- ❖ Herbs and spices: Regular salt.
- ❖ Fish and seafood: Swordfish, shark, mackerel, kingfish, etc.
- ❖ Nuts and Seeds: peanuts, pine nuts, millets, etc.

The Worst Foods to Avoid for Your Thyroid.

These are foods that should be avoided all cost when eating to manage thyroid disorders. They include;

- ❖ Added Sugar: Ice cream, pure chocolate, cotton candy, candies, sugar (brown, white, etc.), pastries, sweets, etc.
- ❖ Refined Grains: White bread, regular pasta, pizza dough, etc.
- ❖ Trans fats: Margarine, sausages, processed meats, etc.
- ❖ Refined Oil: canola oil, cottonseed oil, soybean oil, etc.
- ❖ Highly processed food products

To avoid purchasing these unhealthy foods mistakenly, you have to scrutinize the labels of every packaged food you buy. Some packaged food producers try to trick people by wrongfully tagging their foods 100% natural; however, they cannot lie in the labels of their products. All the ingredients and chemicals used in the manufacturing will be listed in the labels; do well to go through before purchasing.

Advice for Drinks

Excessive consumption of alcohol is known to harm the health in general, the thyroid is not an exception. The Thyroid Healing Diet does not restrict you from consuming alcohol. However, it advises you to also practice moderation.

A single bottle of beer won't harm you, but frequent consumption of a whole bottle of vodka will not just affect your liver but also your thyroid. Studies have shown that alcohol addicts have higher chances of developing hypothyroidism. Therefore, when it comes to alcohol, tread carefully, and practice minimalism.

Chapter 4: Frequently Asked Questions

❖ **Can Thyroid be cured by Diet?**

No, it cannot. The thyroid diet was created to help people manage the health of their thyroid. As it was mentioned several times in the book, the diet is **NOT** a replacement for drugs. It's a lifestyle. It can be followed during drug therapy for effectiveness and maintained after drug therapy.

❖ **Does Thyroid Disorder Affect Breathing?**

Yes, it does. When the gland swells to a certain level (Hyperthyroidism), it presses on the lungs and makes it more difficult to draw breath. On the other hand, hypothyroidism is also known to weaken the respiratory muscles and reduce lung function.

❖ **Are Goitrogenic Foods Bad for Thyroid?**

It depends. Goitrogenic foods are known to cause goiter, but they can not do this single-handedly. Several other requirements have to be satisfied before they are capable of enlarging the thyroid gland. One of such factors is *Iodine deficiency*. If you have a healthy, well-balanced diet, eating goitrogenic foods will only have positive effects on your health. Patients of thyroid disorders are recommended to eat goitrogenic foods in moderation, not completely avoid them. Goitrogens are good for your health. Examples of goitrogenic foods include cabbage, kale, cauliflower, broccoli, spinach, etc.

❖ **Which is more common Hypothyroidism or Hyperthyroidism?**

The most common disorder among all the disorders that affect the thyroid gland is Hypothyroidism. In general, thyroid disorders occur more in women than men. And they have higher rates of occurrence in infants and the elderly.

❖ **Are the ingredients of the Thyroid Healing Diet difficult to purchase?**

No, they are not. The diet does not contain exotic ingredients that can only be purchased by shipping. All the ingredients can be accessed in your local grocery store. When you start researching for new recipes, only choose dishes with ingredients that are easily accessible to you.

❖ **Will I always feel hungry when I start the Thyroid healing diet?**

No, the diet is not designed to keep you hungry or make you lose weight unnecessarily. The purpose of the diet to promote healthy living. When you are constantly hungry, you are not healthy. Keep that in mind when you're considering other diet plans.

Chapter 5: A Healthy 30-day Meal Plan

The Thyroid Healing Diet isn't a treatment plan; it's a lifestyle. Therefore, the meal plan given in this chapter is not designed to help you cure thyroid but to help you kickstart your journey into eating healthy and living healthy. The meal plan was fashioned with the 70 dishes listed in this book. The days are flexible, and the dishes can be rotated among the days as you please.

This is the start of a new chapter in your life, the beginning of watchful eating and structured eating plans. Lots of discipline and determination is required to follow this eating plan and remain loyal after the 30 days are completed. You also have to be ready to comb the internet for more dishes and mix up a couple of them to make your very own recipes.

The key to maintaining this diet is experimentation. If you restrict yourself to the 70 recipes in this book, you're bound to get exhausted and lose the drive to continue with the diet. But if you set a goal of learning 10 new recipes every month, you will be too preoccupied to remember all the processed food and junks you are missing out on.

Let's get started.

Week 1

Day 1

Breakfast: Corn and Salsa Chicken Salad
Snacks: Summer Squash Smoothie

Lunch: Rutabaga Stew with Rice
Snacks: 1 small Orange

Dinner: White Bean Chicken Chili
Dessert: Brazil Nut Brownies

Day 2

Breakfast: Stuffed Banana Peppers

Snacks: Shamrock Shake

Lunch: Pot Roast with Root Vegetables
Snacks: Apple

Dinner: Red Quinoa Salad
Dessert: Strawberry Bruschetta

Day 3

Breakfast: Chicken Salad Adobo
Snacks: Coconut Milk Yogurt

Lunch: Butterflied Cornish Hens with Crush Peppers with Mango and Avocado Wraps
Snacks: Baked Coconut Shrimps

Dinner: Easy Chicken Lasagna
Desserts: Blueberry Smoothie

Day 4

Breakfast: Green Dream Hemp Seed Smoothie
Snacks: Spicy Chicken Wings

Lunch: Channa Saag
Snacks: Broiled Scallops

Dinner: Slow Cooked Barbecue Beef
Desserts: Brazil Nut Brownies

Day 5

Breakfast: Paleo Chicken Soup
Snacks: Deviled Eggs

Lunch: Pasta Fagioli
Snacks: Watermelon Shooter Shots

Dinner: Black Bean Chili
Dessert: Deep-fried Zucchini

Day 6

Breakfast: Spinach with Mushrooms and Leeks
Snacks: Green Juice Popsicles

Lunch: Tuna and Rice Salad
Snacks: Carrot and Apple slaw

Dinner: Grilled Lamb Chops
Dessert: Watermelon Shooter Shots

Breakfast: Swiss Chard and Italian Beans
Snacks: Spicy Chicken Wings

Lunch: Tomato-Curry Lentil Soup
Snacks: Banana Sushi

Dinner: Chili Pronto
Desserts: Mango Fruit Tart

Week 2

Breakfast: Salmon Chowder
Snacks: Summer Squash Smoothie

Lunch: Fiery Fish Tacos
Snacks: Baked Coconut Shrimp

Dinner: Reduced Fat Meatballs
Dessert: Coconut Milk Yogurt

Breakfast: Mussels Mariniere
Snacks: Shamrock Shake

Lunch: Marinated Grilled Shrimp
Snacks: Mango Fruit Tart

Dinner: Eggplant Soup
Dessert: Green Juice Popsicles

Breakfast: Seaweed Salad
Snacks: Strawberry Pineapple Chicken Bites

Lunch: Black-eyed Pea Gumbo
Snacks: Watermelon Shooter Shots

Dinner: Beef and Mushroom Stew
Dessert: Coconut Rice Pudding

Breakfast: Vegetable Tagine with Broiled Scallops
Snacks: Mango Fruit Tart

Lunch: Chicken Cilantro and Cucumber Wraps
Snacks: Green Dream Hemp Seed Smoothie

Dinner: Irish Stew
Dessert: Deep-fried Zucchini

Breakfast: Black Bean Chili
Snacks: Strawberry Pineapple Chicken Bites

Lunch: Pasta Fagioli
Snacks: Mango Fruit Tart

Dinner: Country Beef Stew
Dessert: Spring Fruit Rolls

Breakfast: Green Dream Hemp Seed Smoothie
Snacks: Seaweed Salad

Lunch: Black-eyed Pea Gumbo with Rice and Tuna Salad
Snacks: Marinated Grill Shrimp

Dinner: Chicken, Penne, and Asparagus salad
Dessert: Baked Coconut Shrimp

Breakfast: Coconut Milk Yogurt
Snacks: Mussels Mariniere

Lunch: Easy Chicken Lasagna
Snacks: Summer Squash Smoothie

Dinner: Tarragon Chicken Salad with Jasmine Rice
Dessert: Banana Sushi

Breakfast: Summer Squash Smoothie
Snacks: Spicy Chicken Wings

Lunch: Salmon Chowder with Maple Salmon
Snacks: Deviled Eggs

Dinner: Easy Chili con Queso
Dessert: Honey Chocolate Brownies

Week 3

Day 15

Breakfast: Green Dream Hemp Seed Smoothie
Snacks: Strawberry Bruschetta

Lunch: Marinated Tuna Steak with Guacamole Salad
Snacks: Shamrock Shake

Dinner: Chicken-Prosciutto Bundles with Mediterranean Greek Cucumber Salad
Dessert: Deviled Eggs

Day 16

Breakfast: Seaweed Salad
Snacks: Strawberry Pineapple Chicken Bites

Lunch: Rutabaga Stew with Pasta
Snacks: Banana Sushi

Dinner: Portobello Mushroom and Beans with Chicken Prosciutto Bundles
Dessert: Deviled Eggs

Day 17

Breakfast: White Bean Chicken Chili
Snacks: Coconut Milk Yogurt

Lunch: Vegetable Tagine with Chicken Prosciutto
Snacks: Strawberry Pineapple Chicken Bites

Dinner: Chicken, Cilantro, and Cucumber Wrap
Dessert: Blueberry Smoothie

Day 18

Breakfast: Summer Squash Smoothie
Snacks: Chicken Salad Adobo

Lunch: Tomato-Curry Lentil Stew with Strawberry Bruschetta
Snacks: Strawberry Pineapple Chicken Bites

Dinner: Maple Salmon with Mediterranean Greek Salad

Dessert: Broiled Scallops

Day 19

Breakfast: Seaweed Salad
Snacks: Red Quinoa Salad

Lunch: Grilled Lamb Chops with Watermelon Shooter Shots
Snacks: Carrot and Apple Slaws

Dinner: Country Beef Stew with Strawberry Bruschetta
Dessert: Coconut Rice Pudding

Day 20

Breakfast: Quinoa Porridge
Snacks: Mango Fruit Tart

Lunch: Black Bean Chili with Guacamole Salad
Snacks: Green Juice Popsicles

Dinner: Reduced-Fat Meatballs
Dessert: Strawberry Pineapple Chicken Bites

Day 21

Breakfast: Summer Squash Smoothie
Snacks: Strawberry Bruschetta

Lunch: Grilled Lamb Chops with Red Quinoa Salad
Snacks: Banana Sushi

Dinner: Guacamole Salad with Stuffed Banana Peppers
Desserts: Brazil Nut Brownies

Week 4

Day 22

Breakfast: Slow-Cooked Barbecued Beef as Sandwiches
Snacks: Watermelon Shooter Shakes

Lunch: Guacamole Salad
Snacks: Baked Coconut Shrimps

Dinner: Paleo chicken Soup
Dessert: Fruit Spring Rolls

Day 23

Breakfast: Green Dream Hemp Seed Smoothie
Snacks: Spicy Chicken Wings

Lunch: Swiss Chard and Italian Beans
Snacks: Fruit Spring Rolls

Dinner: Stuffed Banana Peppers with Vegetable Tagine
Dessert: Blueberry Smoothie

Day 24

Breakfast: Channa Saag
Snacks: Shamrock Shake

Lunch: Portobello Mushroom and Shrimps
Snacks: Baked Coconut Shrimps

Dinner: Beef and Mushroom Stew
Dessert: Deviled Eggs

Day 25

Breakfast: Quinoa Porridge
Snacks: Banana Sushi

Lunch: Pot Roast with Root Vegetables
Snacks: Coconut Milk Yogurt

Dinner: Tomato-Curry Lentil Soup
Dessert: Fruit Spring Rolls

Day 26

Breakfast: Cuban Black Beans
Snacks: Strawberry Bruschetta

Lunch: Avocado and Mango Lettuce Wrap with Marinated Tuna Steak
Snacks: Blueberry Smoothie

Dinner: Marinated Tuna Steak
Dessert: Fruit Spring Rolls

Day 27

Breakfast: Green Dream Hemp Seed Smoothie
Snacks: Banana Sushi

Lunch: Corn and Salsa Chicken Salad

Snacks: Coconut Rice Pudding

Dinner: Easy Chicken Lasagna
Dessert: Shrimp Scamp

Day 28

Breakfast: Salmon Chowder
Snacks: Coconut Milk Yogurt

Lunch: Shrimp Scampi with Carrot and Apple Slaw
Snacks: Mango Fruit Tart

Dinner: Split pea Soup
Desserts: Brazil Nut Brownies

Day 29

Breakfast: Orange Zest Chard
Snacks: Shamrock Shake

Lunch: Rice and Tuna Salad
Snacks: Carrot and Apple Slaw

Dinner: Peasant Soup
Desserts: Green Juice Popsicles

Day 30

Breakfast: Quinoa Porridge
Snacks: Summer Squash Smoothie

Lunch: Marinated Tuna Steak
Snacks: Mediterranean Greek Salad

Dinner: Split Pea Soup
Desserts: Deep-fried Zucchini

Chapter 6: Amazing Thyroid Healing Recipes

It is recommended to make all the dishes itemized in this book with fresh, natural, unprocessed foods. Pay attention to the ingredients and nutritional values specified for each dish and plan your meals accordingly. If you do come across a dish that includes one of your forbidden food as an ingredient, skip it and replace it with another recipe in the meal plan.

Combine your diet with exercise and physical activities for optimal health and weight.

Good luck!

Meat Recipes

Slow-Cooked Barbecued Beef

Prep Time: 5 minutes/ Cook Time: 8 hours / Serves: 8

Ingredients:

- 1-1/2 pounds extra-lean ground beef (93% lean)
- 2 Tbsp extra-virgin olive oil
- 2 Tbsp prepared mustard
- 1 cup low-sodium ketchup
- 1 small green bell pepper, chopped
- 3 Tbsp vinegar
- 1/2 tsp ground garlic
- 1 Tbsp Worcestershire sauce
- 1 medium onion, chopped
- 1 tsp chili powder

Directions:

1. Pour the olive oil into a medium skillet and place over medium heat. Once the oil starts to sizzle, add the onions and beef, then *brown* the beef.
2. Pour the rest of the ingredients into a slow cooker. Stir.
3. Add the beef and onions. Stir. Cook on high for 3-4 hours or low for 6-8 hours.
4. Serve as burgers or sandwiches.

Nutritional value per serving:

Calories: 249 kcal, Carbs: 12g Fat: 6g, Protein: 17g.

Grilled Lamb Chops

Prep Time: 120 minutes/ Cook Time: 10 minutes / Serves: 4

Ingredients:

- 2-1/2 pounds of chopped lamb
- 1 tsp of lemon juice
- 1 small lemon
- 2 tsp parsley
- 1 Tbsp Dijon mustard
- 2-1/2 Tbsp salt,

- 1 tsp thyme leaves
- 2 Tbsp oregano
- 2 Tbsp of canola oil
- 3 cloves of garlic
- 2 Tbsp of black pepper
- 3 tsp of extra virgn olive oil

Directions:

1. Preheat the grill to 400°F.
2. Mix the mustard, thyme, parsley, salt, 1 tablespoon oregano, pepper, garlic, olive oil, lemon juice in a medium bowl and stir thoroughly. Set aside one-third of the lemon mixture.
3. Place the lamb in a large baking dish, then pour two-third of the lemon mixture on it. Ensure the lamb is well coated. Allow to marinate in the refrigerator for about 2 hours.
4. Coat the grate of the grill with canola oil. Remove the lamb form the liquid and grill both sices equally for about 10 minutes.
5. Pour the rest of the lemon mixture on the lamb and leave for 5 minutes, then remove.
6. Coat the chops with the leftover oregano. Serve with lemon wedges.

Nutritional value per serving:

Calories: 214kcal, Carbs: 1g Fat: 12g, Protein: 23g

Prep Time: 5 minutes/ Cook Time: 1 hour / Serves: 6

Ingredients:

- 1-1/2 pounds extra-lean ground beef (93% lean)
- 6 oz no-salt-added tomato paste
- 3 medium eggs
- 1/2 tsp ground garlic powder
- 1/2 Tbsp dried oregano
- 1 Tbsp dried parsley
- 4 slices bread, crumbled
- 2 medium onions, chopped
- 1/2 cup Parmesan cheese, grated
- 1/2 cup red wine vinegar
- 1/4 cup of water

Directions:

1. Preheat the oven to 375°F.
2. Mix the beef, cheese, eggs, garlic, oregano, parsley. Whisk well. Add the bread crumbles and form 1-ich meatballs. Arrange the meatballs in a baking pan and bake for 30-40 minutes. Turn only once while baking.
3. Sauté onions in a large skillet, then add tomato paste, vinegar, and water. Cook for 5 minutes then remove from heat.
4. Serve meatballs with tomato sauce. Garnish with fresh parsley (optional).

Nutritional value per serving:

Calories: 457 kcal, Carbs: 28g Fat: 12g, Protein: 32g.

Stuffed Banana Peppers

Prep Time: 10 minutes/ Cook Time: 30 minutes / Serves: 6

Ingredients:

- 1/4 cup all-purpose flour
- 1-pound extra-lean ground beef (93% lean)
- 12 banana peppers, hot or sweet
- 1 small on on, thinly sliced
- 1 medium egg
- 1/2 cup Swiss cheese, grated
- 1/4 tsp black pepper
- 1/4 tsp vegetable oil.

Directions:

5. Preheat the oven to 350°F.
6. Prepare the peppers by washing and cutting off the top and bottom.
7. In a medium skillet, brown the beef and onions. This will take about five minutes. When ready, stir in the cheese.
8. Stuff the beef and cheese mixture into the peppers. Set aside.
9. Pour flour on a chopping board.
10. Mix the egg and black pepper in a separate bowl. Dip the peppers into the egg and then roll in flour to coat. Dip into the egg a second time and then coat in flour again.
11. Coat a baking dish with oil and arrange the peppers in it. Bake for 20 minutes, then remove when the cheese is melted and flour coating turns brown.

Nutritional value per serving:

Calories: 372 kcal, Carbs: 19g Fat: 9g, Protein: 30g.

Pot Roast with Root Vegetables

Prep Time: 5 minutes/ Cook Time: 2 hours / Serves: 8

Ingredients:

- 2-pound beef roast
- 4 turnips, peeled and cut into quarters
- 1 medium onion, chopped into quarters
- 4 potatoes, chopped into quarters
- 6 carrots, chopped
- 2 cups no-salt-added canned tomatoes
- 2 cups low-sodium beef broth
- 1 parsnip, sliced

Directions:

1. Preheat the oven to 350°F.
2. Mix all the ingredients together in a large roasting pan. Place the pan in the oven and bake for 2 hours. Check if the meat is tender. If not, bake for 15 more minutes.
3. Serve.

Nutritional value per serving:

Calories: 527 kcal, Carbs: 41g Fat: 22g, Protein: 40g.

Country Beef Stew

Prep Time: 5 minutes/ Cook Time: 2 hours / Serves: 8

Ingredients:

- 2-pound boneless beef chuck, cut into 1-inch cubes
- 2 medium carrot, sliced
- 2 Tbsp extra-virgin olive oil
- 1 medium onion, chopped
- 1-1/2 cups water
- 1 Tbsp Worcestershire sauce
- 3/4 tsp tarragon
- 1/2 tsp black pepper
- 2 cups canned no-salt-added tomatoes
- 1 clove garlic, minced

Directions:

1. In a medium skillet, *brown* half of the beef. This will take about five minutes.
2. Remove the beef carefully, then brown the other half of the beef. Once done, join both browned beef together in the skillet.
3. Stir in the water, Worcestershire sauce, tomatoes, onions, tarragon, garlic, and black pepper. Bring to a boil.
4. Lower the heat and allow to simmer, covered, for about an hour. Add carrots, simmer for 20 minutes, then increase the heat and add beans. Cook for 5 minutes.
5. Serve.

Nutritional value per serving:

Calories: 587 kcal, Carbs: 42g Fat: 26g, Protein: 46g.

Prep Time: 5 minutes/ Cook Time: 1 hor 30 minutes/ Serves: 8

Ingredients:

- 2 pounds beef stew meat
- 1/4 cup cornstarch
- 4 potatoes, cut into quarters
- 1 cup medium onion, sliced
- 12 oz dark beer
- 1/2 cup of water
- 2 cups beef broth
- 3 Tbsp no-salt-added tomato paste
- 1 clove garlic, minced
- 2 medium carrot, sliced
- 2 turnips, cut into quarters
- 1 tsp rosemary
- 1/4 tsp black pepper, grounded
- 2 bay leaves

Directions:

1. Pour all the ingredients (except cornstarch and water) into a pot and cook until meat and potatoes are tender. This may take up to an hour
2. Mix the cornstarch and water in a bowl, then add to the pot of stew. Cook for about 30 minutes, until the soup is well thickened.
3. Serve.

Nutritional value per serving:

Calories: 420 kcal, Carbs: 43g Fat: 12g, Protein: 43g.

Eggplant Stew

Prep Time: 5 minutes/ Cook Time: 1 hour / Serves: 6

Ingredients:

- 1-1/2 pounds beef stew meat, cubed
- 2 Tbsp extra-virgin olive oil
- 2 cups no-salt-added canned tomatoes
- 1 medium onion, chopped
- 1/2 tsp oregano
- 1/2 tsp basil
- 1/2 tsp cumin
- 1/4 tsp red pepper flakes
- 1/2 tsp garlic powder
- 1 cup of water
- 2 Tbsp no-salt-added tomato paste
- 1 cup white wine
- 1 potato, peeled and cubed
- 1 eggplant, peeled and cubed
- 2 mushrooms, sliced

Directions:

1. In a medium skillet, *brown* half of the beef. This will take about five minutes.
2. Remove the beef carefully, then brown the other half of the beef. Once done, drain the oil and join both browned beef together in the skillet.
3. Stir in water, tomato paste, tomatoes, onions, and spice. Bring to a boil.
4. Lower the heat, keep covered and simmer for 45 minutes.
5. Add potatoes and wine, stir and keep simmering for 10 more minutes.
6. Add in the cubed eggplants and mushrooms. Simmer for 20 minutes and remove from heat.
7. Serve.

Nutritional value per serving:

Calories: 504 kcal, Carbs: 23g Fat: 27g, Protein: 36g.

Prep Time: - minutes/ Cook Time: 45 minutes / Serves: 6

Ingredients:

- 1-pound roast beef, chopped
- 2 cups beef broth
- 1/2 cup turnips, cubed
- 1-pound canned mixed vegetables
- 1 cup canned no-salt-added tomatoes

Directions:

1. Mix all the ingredients in a large pot and place over low heat. Simmer for 45 minutes until vegetables are tender.
2. Serve.

Nutritional value per serving:

Calories: 198 kcal, Carbs: 13g Fat: 5g, Protein: 25g.

Beef and Mushroom Stew

Prep Time: 5 minutes/ Cook Time: 1 hour / Serves: 6

Ingredients:

- 2 cups canned no-salt-added tomatoes
- 14 oz beef broth
- 1/2 cup red wine
- 1/4 tsp ground black pepper
- 5 medium potatoes, quartered
- 3 medium carrots, sliced
- 2 mushrooms, sliced
- 1 bay leaf
- 1/4 tsp dried rosemary
- 3 Tbsp flour
- 1/4 cup of water
- 1-1/2 pounds beef round steak, cut into cubes

Directions:

1. Mix all the ingredients (except flour, tomatoes and water) in a large pot and place over medium heat. Cover and cook for 1 hour.
2. Mix the flour, water and tomatoes in a small bowl.
3. Add tomatoes mixture to the pot. Cook until stew starts to thicken. This may take about 10-20 minutes
4. Serve.

Nutritional value per serving:

Calories: 507 kcal, Carbs: 59g Fat: 7g, Protein: 50g.

Chicken & Poultry Recipes

Corn and Salsa Chicken Salad

Prep Time: 5 minutes/ Cook Time: 10 minutes / Serves: 4

Ingredients:

- 4 chicken breast halves
- 1/2 cup salsa
- 2 Tbsp balsamic vinegar
- 8 fat-free tortilla chips, crushed
- 1 tsp brown mustard
- 1 Tbsp Cajun seasoning powder
- 1 tomato, sliced

- 2 Tbsp fresh cilantro, chopped
- 2 cups fresh corn kernels
- 1 small avocado, peeled, pitted and chopped
- 4 scallions, chopped
- Non-stick spray

Directions:

1. Season the chicken with Cajun seasoning powder.
2. Place a large skillet over medium heat and coat with non-stick spray
3. Place the chicken in the skillet and cook until both sides turn brown. This will take about 5 minutes for each side.
4. Cut each chicken into 4 slices, keeping the slices joined at one end.
5. Prepare the dressing by mixing the salsa, 1 Tbsp cilantro, vinegar, and mustard in a bowl.
6. Prepare the salad by mixing the scallions, avocados, tomatoes, corn and leftover 1 Tbsp cilantro in a large bowl. Dribble the dressing over it and toss.
7. Serve the salad into 4 plates with a chicken on each plate.

Nutritional value per serving:

Calories: 269 kcal, Carbs: 24g Fat: 8g, Protein: 29g.

Chicken, Penne, and Asparagus Salad

Prep Time: 5 minutes/ Cook Time: 30 minutes / Serves: 4

Ingredients:

- 1/2 pounc chicken breasts, cut into strips
- 2 tsp poultry and meat seasoning
- 1-pound gluten-free pasta
- 1-pound asparagus, chopped
- 2 medium tomatoes, sliced
- 1 cup fresh basil, chopped
- 1/4 cup Pecorino Romano cheese, grated
- 2 cloves of garlic, minced
- 1 Tbsp extra virgin olive oil
- 1/4 tsp salt
- Non-stick spray

Directions:

1. Rub the chicken with the seasoning.
2. Place a large skillet over medium heat and coat with non-stick spray
3. Place the chicken in the skillet and cook until both sides turn brown. This wil take about 5 minutes for each side.
4. Boil the pasta on another burner. Add salt if desired. Once ready, drain the pasta into a colander and reserve the cooking water. Rinse the drained pasta in cold water then transfer it to a bowl
5. In the pasta cooking water, add the asparagus and cook until tender (about 3 minutes). Once done, rinse in cold water and mix with the pasta.
6. In the bowl containing the pasta and asparagus, add the tomatoes, garlic, cheese, oil, salt, basil and chicken. Toss until well combined.
7. Serve.

Nutritional value per serving:

Calories: 273 kcal, Carbs: 29g Fat: 8g, Protein: 21g.

Chicken Salad Adobo

Prep Time: 5 minutes/ Cook Time: 10 minutes / Serves: 6

Ingredients:

- 1 Tbsp orange zest, grated
- 2 Tbsp orange juice, squeezed
- 1 Tbsp white wine vinegar
- 2 tsp extra virgin olive oil
- 1 tsp honey
- 1 large tomato, sliced
- 1 tsp Dijon mustard
- 1 clove of garlic, minced
- 1 Tbsp adobo seasoning
- 1/8 tsp salt

- 1 red bell pepper, chopped
- 1-pound chicken thighs, skinless, deboned and cut into pieces
- 15-1/2 oz black beans, drained and rinsed
- 1 ripe mango, diced
- 1 small red onion, thinly sliced
- 1/2 cup fresh cilantro, chopped
- 1 jalapeño pepper, seeded and chopped
- Non-stick spray

Directions:

1. Rub the chicken with the adobo seasoning.
2. Place a large skillet over medium heat and coat with non-stick spray
3. Place the chicken in the skillet and cook until both sides turn brown. This will take about 5 minutes for each side. Remove from skillet and keep in a bowl.
4. Prepare the dressing by mixing the orange juice, orange zest, extra virgin olive oil, vinegar, honey, garlic, mustard, and salt in a small bowl until well-combined blended.
5. In the bowl with the chicken, add the mango, beans, bell pepper, tomatoes, cilantro, onions and jalapeño. Drizzle the dressing over the salad and toss until well-combined.
6. Serve.

Nutritional value per serving:

Calories: 248kcal, Carbs: 23g Fat: 8g, Protein: 21g.

THYROID HEALING DIET

Butterflied Cornish Hens with Crushed Pepper and Garlic

Prep Time: 5 minutes/ Cook Time: 30 minutes / Serves: 4

Ingredients:

- 1 Tbsp fresh flat-leaf parsley, chopped
- 2 tsp extra virgin olive oil non-stick spray
- 1 large clove of garlic, minced
- 1/2 tsp salt
- 1/2 tsp red pepper flakes
- 3-pound Cornish game hen

Directions:

1. Preheat the outdoor grill
2. Lightly oil the grate of the grill with olive oil nonstick spray.
3. Mix all the ingredients (except the Cornish hen) in a small bowl.
4. Prepare the hen by dissecting with kitchen shears. Cut along both sides of the hens, remove the backbones and discard. Then rub the parsley mixture all over the chicken and under the skin too.
5. Place the hen on the grate and grill for about 30 minutes until both sides are crisp and golden. Remove the hen and place on a chopping board.
6. Chop the grilled chicken into large pieces. Serve.

Nutritional value per serving:

Calories: 224kcal, Carbs: 1g Fat: 8g, Protein: 35g

Easy Chicken Lasagna

Prep Time: 5 minutes/ Cook Time: 1 hour 15 minutes / Serves: 9

Ingredients:

- 1-pound chicken breast, shredded
- 1/2 pound white mushrooms, thinly sliced
- 26 oz fat-free marinara sauce
- 2 large egg whites, lightly whisked
- 16 oz part-skim mozzarella cheese, shredded
- 1/4 cup Parmigiano-Reggiano cheese, grated
- 1/2 tsp fresh nutmeg, grated
- 8 oz no-salt-added tomato sauce
- 15 oz fat-free ricotta cheese
- 9 oz no-boil lasagna noodles
- Non-stick spray

Directions:

1. Preheat the oven to 375°F.
2. Spray the non-stick spray on a large saucepan and place over medium heat. Add the chicken and cook until all sides are lightly browned. This may take 3-4 minutes.
3. Add in the mushrooms. Cook until the liquid comes out or for 5 minutes.
4. Pour in the marina sauce, stir, lower the heat and allow to simmer. Set the pot aside
5. Mix the mozzarella and ricotta cheese, nutmeg, and egg whites in a small bowl. Set aside.
6. Spread the tomato sauce mixture smoothly on the bottom of a baking pan. Arrange 5 lasagna noodles over the sauce in the first layer. Add 1/3 of the chicken mixture.
7. Repeat step 6 until the ingredients are exhausted. (The ingredients listed above will only make 3 layers).
8. Sprinkle Parmigiano-Reggiano on top of the lasagna, cover, then bake for 45 minutes.
9. Uncover, then bake until the top turns slightly brown. This may take about 10 minutes.
10. Allow cooling for 5 minutes before serving.

Nutritional value per serving:

Calories: 340kcal, Carbs: 36g Fat: 7g, Protein: 33g.

Chili Pronto

Prep Time: 5 minutes/ Cook Time: 30 minutes / Serves: 4

Ingredients:

- 14-1/2 tomatoes with green chiles, diced
- 2 green bell peppers, diced
- 9 0z can mixed vegetables
- 4-1/2 can chopped mild green chiles
- 1 Tbsp chili seasoning mix
- 1-1/2 cups cooked chicken, chopped
- 1/4 cup fat-free sour cream
- 2 scallions, thinly sliced and white and green part only
- 2 cups of baked tortilla chips

Directions:

1. Mix the bell peppers, tomatoes, mixed vegetables, chili seasoning, and chiles in a medium saucepan. Cover and bring to a boil.
2. Lower the heat, uncover, and allow to simmer until the vegetables soften and the flavors are blended. This may take about 10 minutes.
3. Add the chicken and cook for 3 minutes. Stir periodically.
4. Split the chili into 4 small bowls. Drizzle the sour cream on the top and garnish with scallions.
5. Serve with tortilla chips.

Nutritional value per serving:

Calories: 235kcal, Carbs: 30g Fat: 4g, Protein: 20g

Easy Chili con Queso

Prep Time: 5 minutes/ Cook Time: 30 minutes / Serves: 4

Ingredients:

- 1 tsp extra virgin olive oil
- 2 tsp chili seasoning mix
- 14 oz canned tomatoes, diced
- 1 large onion, chopped
- 2 cups corn kernels
- 1 cup cooked chicken, chopped
- 4 flour tortillas, 6 inches each
- 1/2 cup reduced-fat Monterey Jack cheese, shredded

Directions:

1. Add the oil to a large saucepan, then place over medium heat.
2. Add the onions to the oil and fry until translucent. This will take about 2 minutes.
3. Add the seasoning mix and cook until the aroma fills the air. Add tomatoes and boil.
4. Once boiled, lower the heat, uncover, and simmer for about three minutes. Stir in the chicken and corn. Continue to simmer for 3 minutes. Set aside.
5. Spray the non-stick spray on a large skillet and place over medium heat. Add in the tortillas separately, and cook each side for 1 minute. Cut each tortilla into shapes (usually triangles)
6. Add cheese to the chili sauce and stir until it melts completely.
7. Serve the chili with toasted tortilla triangles.

Nutritional value per serving:

Calories: 290kcal, Carbs: 36g Fat: 9g, Protein: 19g.

Tarragon Chicken Salad with Orange Mayonnaise

Prep Time: 10 minutes/ Cook Time: 0 minutes / Serves: 4

Ingredients:

- 2 tsp tarragon, chopped
- 1-1/2 tsp Dijon mustard
- 1-1/2 tsp apple cider vinegar
- 1 cup seedless green grapes, halved
- 1/4 tsp salt
- 1/8 tsp black pepper
- 2 cups shredded cooked chicken breast
- 8 Boston lettuce leaves
- 1 celery stalk, thinly sliced
- 1/4 cup fat-free mayonnaise
- 1/4 cup red onion, thinly sliced
- 1 navel orange
- 2 Tbsp walnuts, chopped

Directions:

1. Prepare the dressing by mixing the mayonnaise, mustard, salt, vinegar, tarragon, and pepper in a medium bowl. Grate about 1/2 teaspoon orange zest and add to the dressing.
2. Peel and deseed the orange, then cut into 4 quarters.
3. Add the orange quarters, grapes, chicken, celery, walnuts, and onion into the dressing. Toss until well-combined.
4. Share the lettuce into four equal parts. Spoon the mixed salad onto the lettuce. Serve.

Nutritional value per serving:

Calories: 183kcal, Carbs: 15g Fat: 6g, Protein: 19g.

Chicken-Prosciutto Bundles

Prep Time: 5 minutes/ Cook Time: 50 minutes / Serves: 4

Ingredients:

- 4 chicken breasts
- 1 tsp extra virgin olive oil
- 1/4 tsp black pepper
- 4 slices of part-skim mozzarella cheese
- 12 basil leaves
- 8 thin slices prosciutto

Directions:

1. Preheat the oven and set to 400°F.
2. Make pockets on the side of each chicken by gently slicing the meat. Do not cut to reach the other side. Insert a slice of cheese and 3 basil leaves into each pocket. Sprinkle pepper on each chicken and wrap in 2 slices of prosciutto.
3. Add the olive oil to a large skillet, then place on medium-high heat. Add the chicken and fry until lightly browned. This will take about 5-6 minutes.
4. Remove the chicken from the skillet and place in the oven to bake for 15 minutes.
5. Remove from oven. Cool.
6. Serve.

Nutritional value per serving:

Calories: 267kcal, Carbs: 1g Fat: 10g, Protein: 40g.

Chicken, Cilantro, and Cucumber Wraps

Prep Time: 5 minutes/ Cook Time: 30 minutes / Serves: 4

Ingredients:

- 2 cups shredded cooked chicken breast
- 1/4 cup low-fat mayonnaise
- 1 tsp ginger, minced
- 1/4 cup cilantro, chopped
- 4 flour tortillas, 8 inches
- 1 tsp dark sesame oil
- 1/4 tsp salt
- 1 medium cucumber, diced
- 1/4 tsp black pepper

Directions:

1. Mix the cucumber, mayonnaise, chicken, cilantro, ginger, salt, oil, and pepper in a medium bowl. Toss until well combined. Set aside for 10 minutes to allow flavors to blend.
2. Place a large non-stick skillet over medium heat and toast the tortillas. Make sure both sides are accounted for. Remove from heat after 2 minutes.
3. Share the chicken filling equally among the tortillas and roll them up. Divide the rolls into equal halves.
4. Serve.

Nutritional value per serving:

Calories: 239kcal, Carbs: 21g Fat: 6g, Protein: 24g.

Fish & Seafood Recipes

Mussels Mariniere

Prep Time: 15 minutes/ Cook Time: 35 minutes / Serves: 4

Ingredients:

- 4 quarts mussels, debearded and cleaned
- 2 cloves of garlic, minced
- 1 small onion, chopped
- 6 Tbsp fresh parsley, chopped
- 1 bay leaf
- 1/4 tsp dried thyme
- 2 cups white wine
- 3 Tbsp cream cheese, divided

Directions:

1. Mix the wine, onion, thyme, garlic, 2 Tbsp cream cheese, 4 Tbsp parsley and bay leaf in a large pot and place over medium heat. Bring to a boil
2. Reduce the heat and simmer for 2 minutes before adding the mussels.
3. After mussels, cook until shells open. This will take about 4-5 minutes
4. Remove mussels, drain liquid and set aside.
5. Add leftover cream cheese and parsley to the sauce in the pot. Cook until melts itcompletely.
6. Serve mussels into plates and dribble the prepared sauce over it.

Nutritional value per serving:

Calories: 298kcal, Carbs: 11g Fat: 10g, Protein: 19g.

Marinated Tuna Steak

Prep Time: 40 minutes/ Cook Time: 11 minutes / Serves: 4

Ingredients:

- 4 tuna steaks (4 oz each)
- 1/4 cup of orange juice
- 1/4 cup Worcestershire sauce
- 2 Tbsp extra virgin olive oil
- 1 Tbsp lemon juice
- 2 Tbsp fresh parsley, chopped
- 1 clove garlic, minced
- 1/2 tsp chopped fresh oregano
- 1/2 tsp ground black pepper

Directions:

1. Prepare the marinade by mixing all the ingredients except the tuna in a medium bowl. Mix until well combined, then add the tuna steaks and coat all sides. Leave in the refrigerator for 30 minutes to marinade.
2. While waiting, preheat the grill and lightly oil the grates.
3. Remove tuna and marinade from the refrigerator. Arrange tuna steaks on the grates and grill. Cook for 5 minutes, then turn tuna steaks and coat with marinade. Turn the tuna periodically and baste with marinade until steak is grilled to the desired level. Discard leftover marinade
4. Serve.

Nutritional value per serving:

Calories: 200 kcal. Carbs: 4g Fat: 8g, Protein: 28g.

Maple Salmon

Prep Time: 40 minutes/ Cook Time: 20 minutes / Serves: 4

Ingredients:

- 2 Tbsp Worcestershire sauce
- 1/4 cup maple syrup
- 1 clove of garlic, thinly sliced
- 1/8 tsp ground black pepper
- 1/4 tsp garlic salt
- 1-pound salmon

Directions:

1. Preheat the oven to 400°F
2. Mix the syrup, sauce, garlic, pepper, and garlic salt in a small bowl
3. Arrange the salmon in a baking dish and cover with maple marinade. Cover and keep tuna in the refrigerator for 30 minutes to marinate.
4. Remove salmon from refrigerator and place in the oven to bake for 20 minutes or until it can be flaked with a fork
5. Allow to cool then serve.

Nutritional value per serving:

Calories: 265 kcal, Carbs: 14g Fat: 12g, Protein: 23g.

Marinated Grilled Shrimp

Prep Time: 35 minutes/ Cook Time:6 minutes / Serves: 6

Ingredients:

- 3 cloves of garlic, minced
- 1/3 cup extra virgin olive oil
- 1/4 cup tomato sauce
- 2 Tbsp red wine vinegar
- 2 Tbsp fresh basil, chopped
- 1/2 tsp salt
- 1/4 tsp cayenne pepper
- 2 pounds fresh shrimp, deveined and peeled
- Skewers

Directions:

1. Preheat the grill
2. Mix all the ingredients together in a large bowl. Make sure the shrimp is well coated. Cover and keep in the refrigerator for about 30 minutes to 1 hour. Stir only once.
3. Arrange shrimp on skewers by piercing through from the tail to the head. Discard leftover marinade
4. Lightly oil the grates of the grill and arrange shrimps on it. Grill both sides until shrimp turn opaque. This may take about 5-6 minutes.
5. Serve.

Nutritional value per serving:

Calories: 273 kcal, Carbs: 3g Fat: 7g, Protein: 41g.

Shrimp Scampi

Prep Time: 15 minutes/ Cook Time: 10 minutes / Serves: 6

Ingredients:

- 8 oz packaged gluten-free pasta
- 1/2 cup cream cheese
- 4 cloves of garlic, minced
- 1/4 tsp salt
- 1-pound shrimp, deveined and peeled
- 1 cup dry white wine
- 1/4 tsp ground black pepper
- 3/4 cup Parmesan cheese
- 1 Tbsp fresh parsley, chopped

Directions:

1. Boil the gluten-free pasta and pour into a colander when ready.
2. Melt the cream cheese in a large saucepan placed over medium heat. Add the shrimp and garlic, fry for 5 minutes or until both side of the garlic are done.
3. Pour the white wine into the saucepan, add pepper, then boil.
4. Transfer the shrimp to a bowl then mix with the drained pasta.
5. Serve into plates and garnish with cheese and parsley.

Nutritional value per serving:

Calories: 606 kcal, Carbs: 36g Fat:30g, Protein: 36g.

Fiery Fish Tacos with Crunchy Corn Salsa

Prep Time: 30 minutes/ Cook Time: 10 minutes / Serves: 6

Ingredients:

- 1 small red onion, diced
- 1 cup jicama, peeled and diced
- 1/2 cup red bell pepper, diced
- 1 cup cilantro leaves, chopped
- 1 small lime, zested and juiced
- 2 Tbsp cayenne pepper,
- 1 Tbsp ground black pepper
- 2 Tbsp salt,
- 6 fillets tilapia, 4 oz each
- 2 Tbsp extra virgin olive oil
- 12 corn tortillas, lightly heated
- 2 Tbsp sour cream

Directions:

1. Preheat the grill and lightly oil the grates.
2. Mix the corn, onion, bell pepper, cilantro, lime juice, zest and jicama together in a medium bowl. This will serve as the corn salsa
3. In another bowl, mix cayenne pepper, salt, black pepper and olive oil. This will serve as the *glaze*.
4. Brush the glaze on each fillet. Make sure both sides are coated
5. Arrange the fillets on the grate and grill for 3 minutes on each side.
6. For a serving, arrange a fillet, corn salsa, and sour cream on two corn tortillas.

Nutritional value per serving:

Calories: 351 kcal, Carbs: 40g Fat:10g, Protein: 29g.

Salmon Chowder

Prep Time: 30 minutes/ Cook Time: 10 minutes / Serves: 8

Ingredients:

- 3 Tbsp cream cheese
- 2 cups chicken broth
- 1 tsp ground garlic
- 2medium potatoes, diced
- 15 oz can creamed corn
- carrots, sliced
- 1 tsp salt
- 1 tsp ground black pepper
- 1/2 cup celery, chopped
- 1 tsp dried dill weed
- 2 medium onions, chopped
- 2 canned salmon, 16 ounces each
- 12 oz evaporated milk
- 1/2-pound Cheddar cheese, shredded

Directions:

1. Use cream cheese to sauté onions, garlic and celery until onions turn translucent.
2. Stir in broth, potatoes, potatoes, carrots, pepper, salt, and dill. Bring to a boil, then lower heat and simmer for 20 minutes.
3. Add salmon, milk, corn and cheese. Wait until cheese melts completely, then remove from heat. Serve.

Nutritional value per serving:

Calories: 490 kcal, Carbs: 27g Fat: 26, Protein: 29g.

THYROID HEALING DIET

Baked Coconut Shrimp

Prep Time: 15 minutes/ Cook Time: 15 minutes / Serves: 4

Ingredients:

- 1-pound large shrimp, deveined and peeled
- 1 tsp salt
- 3/4 tsp cayenne pepper
- 2 cups sweetened coconut flakes
- 3 egg whites, beaten until foamy
- 1/3 cup cornstarch

Directions:

1. Preheat oven to 400°F. Coat baking sheet with non-stick spray.
2. In a small bowl, mix cornstarch, cayenne pepper, and salt. Set aside.
3. Pour the coconut flakes into a separate bowl and set aside.
4. Wash the shrimps, then dry with paper towels. Coat each shrimp one at a time by dredging in cornstarch mixture, then dipping it into the egg foam before finally rolling it on the coconut flakes. Make sure each shrimp is well coated before arranging them on the prepared baking sheet.
5. Bake until shrimps turn pink and coconut is browned. This will take about 15-20 minutes. Remember to flip shrimps after 10 minutes.
6. Allow to cool, then serve.

Nutritional value per serving:

Calories: 310 kcal, Carbs: 27g Fat: 11, Protein: 22g.

Broiled Scallops

Prep Time: 5 minutes/ Cook Time: 8 minutes / Serves: 3

Ingredients:

- 1-1/2 pounds of bay scallops
- 1 tsp garlic salt
- 2 Tbsp cream cheese, melted
- 2 Tbsp lemon juice

Directions:

1. Switch on the broiler.
2. Rinse scallop and arrange in baking pan. Sprinkle with garlic salt, lemon juice and cream cheese.
3. Broil for 6-8 minutes and remove from oven when scallops turn golden.
4. Serve with melted cream cheese on the side for dipping.

Nutritional value per serving:

Calories: 273 kcal, Carbs: 7g Fat: 9, Protein: 38g.

Rice and Tuna Salad

Prep Time: 1 hour 10 minutes/ Cook Time: 0 minutes / Serves: 6

Ingredients:

- 2 cup white rice, cooked
- 1 can (5 oz) of tuna, drained
- 1 can (8 oz) of sweet corn, drained
- 2 Tbsp sweet pickle relish
- 1/2 cup creamy salad dressing

Directions:

1. Pour the cooked rice into a large bowl.
2. Add the tuna, sweet corn, pickle, and salad dressing. Toss, then refrigerate for 1 hour.
3. Serve.

Nutritional value per serving:

Calories: 234 kca , Carbs: 36g Fat: 6, Protein: 9g.

Vegan & Vegetarian Recipes

Quinoa Porridge

Prep Time: 5 minutes/ Cook Time: 15 minutes / Serves: 4

Ingredients:

- 2 cups organic quinoa, white
- 1 tsp vanilla extract, pure
- 1 tsp ground turmeric
- 1 tsp ground cinnamon
- 2 cups coconut milk, preferably unsweetened
- 1/2 tsp ground ginger
- 1/8 tsp black pepper
- 1/2 cup canned pears, diced and with juice
- 1/8 tsp salt
- 1/4 coconut flakes, preferably unsweetened
- 1/2 cup golden raisins

Directions:

1. Pour the quinoa into a bowl and rinse under cold water.
2. In a medium-sized saucepan, mix the quinoa and coconut milk and place over medium heat to boil.
3. Once the mixture starts boiling, reduce the heat and cover the saucepan with a tight-fitting lid. Cook for 10-15 minutes until the porridge thickens and most of the milk is absorbed
4. Remove the pan from heat and add the rest of the ***Ingredients:*** turmeric, vanilla, cinnamon, black pepper, ginger, and salt, then stir.
5. For toppings, add pears, coconut flakes, and raisins as desired

Nutritional value per serving:

Calories: 276 kcal, Carbs: 48g Fat: 2g, Protein: 6g.

Channa Saag

Prep Time: 5 minutes/ Cook Time: 12 minutes / Serves: 2

Ingredients:

- 2/3 cup dried beans
- 1-1/2 cups cooked no-salt-added garbanzo beans
- 12 oz spinach, chopped
- 1 tsp ground cinnamon
- 1 tsp ground coriander
- 1 tsp ground cardamom
- 1 tsp garam marsala
- 1 medium onion, thinly sliced
- 2 medium tomatoes, sliced
- 2 cloves of garlic, minced
- 1 tsp ginger, grated
- 3 Tbsp water

Directions:

1. Add 3 tablespoons of water to a large saucepan, then place on medium heat
2. Add the onions, ginger, and garlic to the water and cook until tender. This will take about 2 minutes.
3. Add the spinach, spices, and tomatoes. Stir, then allow to cook for 5 minutes
4. Stir in the cayenne pepper and chickpeas. Cook for 5 minutes.
5. Serve.

Nutritional value per serving:

Calories: 298kcal, Carbs: 53g Fat: 4.3g, Protein: 21g.

Portobello Mushroom and Beans

Prep Time: 5 minutes/ Cook Time: 12 minutes / Serves: 2

Ingredients:

- 1 medium onion, thinly sliced
- 2/3 cup dried beans
- 2 large portobello mushroom caps, sliced
- 1-1/2 cups cooked no-salt-added garbanzo beans
- 1 large tomato, sliced
- 2 cloves of garlic, minced
- 1/2 cup vegetable broth
- 3 Tbsp water

Directions:

1. Add 3 tablespoons of water to a large saucepan, then place on medium heat.
2. Add the onions and garlic to the water and cook until tender. This will take about 2 minutes.
3. Add the broth and mushroom. Stir, then allow to cook for 5 minutes until mushrooms become tender.
4. Stir in the garbanzo beans and tomatoes. Reduce the heat and simmer for 5 minutes.
5. Serve.

Nutritional value per serving:

Calories: 143kcal, Carbs: 25g Fat: 2.1g, Protein: 11g.

Cuban Black Beans

Prep Time: 5 minutes/ Cook Time: 35 minutes / Serves: 4

Ingredients:

- 1 medium green bell pepper
- 4-1/4 cocked no-salt-added black beans
- 2 cups no-salt-added tomato juice
- 1 cup no-salt-added tomato sauce
- 4 cloves of garlic, minced
- 1 tsp cumin
- 1/2 tsp ginger powder
- 1/3 tsp ground black pepper
- 1/3 cup cilantro
- 1 Tbsp red wine vinegar
- 1-1/2 cup dried beans
- 1 Tbsp water

Directions:

1. Add 1 tablespoon of water to a large saucepan, then place on medium heat.
2. Add the onions and bell pepper to the water and cook until tender. This will take about 2 minutes.
3. Add the rest of the ingredients except cilantro and vinegar. Allow to boil, then cover and reduce the heat. Allow to simmer for 25 minutes then stir in the cilantro and vinegar.
4. Serve.

Nutritional value per serving:

Calories: 255kcal, Carbs: 46g Fat: 3g, Protein: 15g.

Prep Time: 10 minutes/ Cook Time: 0 minutes / Serves: 2

Ingredients:

- 1 medium mango, diced
- 1 medium tomato, chopped
- 1 large ripe avocado, peeled and pitted
- 1 medium cucumber, diced and peeled
- 1 Tbsp lime juice
- 6 leaves of romaine lettuce (or collard green)

Directions:

1. Mash the avocado to form cream cheese in a bowl. Add in the diced mango, tomato, cucumber, and lime juice, then mix.
2. Spread the avocado cream cheese mixture on each of the lettuce leaves and roll to form a wrap.
3. Serve

Nutritional value per serving:

Calories: 281kcal, Carbs: 36g Fat: 16g, Protein: 8g.

Vegetable Tagine

Prep Time: 10 minutes/ Cook Time: 1 hour / Serves: 4

Ingredients:

- 1 large onion, thinly sliced
- 2 medium carrots, diced
- 1 medium red bell pepper, chopped
- 1 tsp cinnamon
- 1 tsp turmeric
- 2 medium tomatoes, diced
- 1/2 dried apricot
- 1 large tomato, sliced
- 1 clove of garlic, minced
- 1/2 cup no-salt-added vegetable broth
- 1 cup of water
- 1 medium zucchini, diced
- 1 Tbsp lemon juice
- 1/2 cup dried beans
- 2 Tbsp cilantro, minced
- 1-1/2 garbanzo beans, cooked

Directions:

1. Soak the apricots in hot water for 20 minutes. Add enough water to cover.
2. Pour the 1 cup of water into a large saucepan and place over medium heat. Add the bell pepper, carrots and onion. Cover and bring to a boil.
3. Once boiled, stir in the zucchini, cinnamon, tomatoes, turmeric, garlic, and vegetable broth. Lower the heat and simmer for 25 minutes.
4. Drain the apricots, chop, then add to the pan. Also add the soaking water, lemon juice, raisins, and garbanzo beans. Cook for 5 minutes.
5. Add the cilantro. Stir.
6. Serve.

Nutritional value per serving:

Calories: 242kcal, Carbs: 48g Fat: 2.9g, Protein: 12g.

Orange Zest Chard

Prep Time: 5 minutes/ Cook Time: 10 minutes / Serves: 4

Ingredients:

- 2 shallots, chopped
- 2 cloves of garlic, minced
- 1 medium orange, juiced and zested
- 2 bunches of Swiss chard, leaves and stem separated and chopped
- 1/4 tsp allspice
- 1/4 tsp chipotle chili flakes
- 2 Tbsp blood orange vinegar

Directions:

1. Stir-fry the garlic, shallots, and chard stems in a non-stick pan for about 5 minutes. Stir continuously to avoid burning.
2. Add the orange juice and zest, chili flakes, and allspice.
3. Deglaze the pan with vinegar, then add the chard leaves. Steam for about 3 minutes.
4. Serve.

Nutritional value per serving:

Calories: 35kcal, Carbs: 7g Fat: 0.2g, Protein: 2g.

Seaweed Salad

Prep Time: 10 minutes/ Cook Time: - minutes / Serves: 4

Ingredients:

- 3/4 oz dried wakame seaweed, cut
- 3 Tbsp rice vinegar, unseasoned
- 3 Tbsp Worcestershire sauce
- 1 Tbsp sesame oil
- Red pepper flakes
- 1 tsp ginger, grated
- 1/2 tsp garlic, minced
- 2 scallions, thinly sliced
- 1/4 cup of carrots, shredded
- 2 Tbsp cilantro, chopped
- 1 Tbsp sesame seeds, toasted

Directions:

1. Prepare warm water in a medium bowl and soak the sea weed in it for 5 minutes. Make sure the bowl is covered.
2. Remove the seaweed from the soaking water and rinse. Be sure to squeeze out any excess water.
3. In a separate bowl, mix the vinegar, sesame oil, soy sauce, pepper flakes, garlic, and ginger. Then add the squeezed seaweed, carrots, scallions, and cillantro. Toss until well-combined.
4. Sprinkle the sesame seeds on the salad.
5. Serve.

Nutritional value per serving:

Calories: 291kcal, Carbs: 38g Fat: 1.5g, Protein: 19g.

Prep Time: - minutes/ Cook Time: 10 minutes / Serves: 4

Ingredients:

- 6 cloves of garlic, minced
- 1/2 cup dried beans
- 1/2 tsp no-salt Italian seasoning powder
- 1-1/2 cups red kidney beans
- 3 large tomatoes, chopped
- 1-pound Swiss chard
- 1-1/2 tomato sauce, no-salt

Directions:

1. Mix all the ingredients in a pot and place over low heat. Simmer until chard becomes soft. Stir continuously.

Nutritional value per serving:

Calories: 174kcal, Carbs: 34g Fat: 1g, Protein: 13g.

Spinach with Mushrooms and Leeks

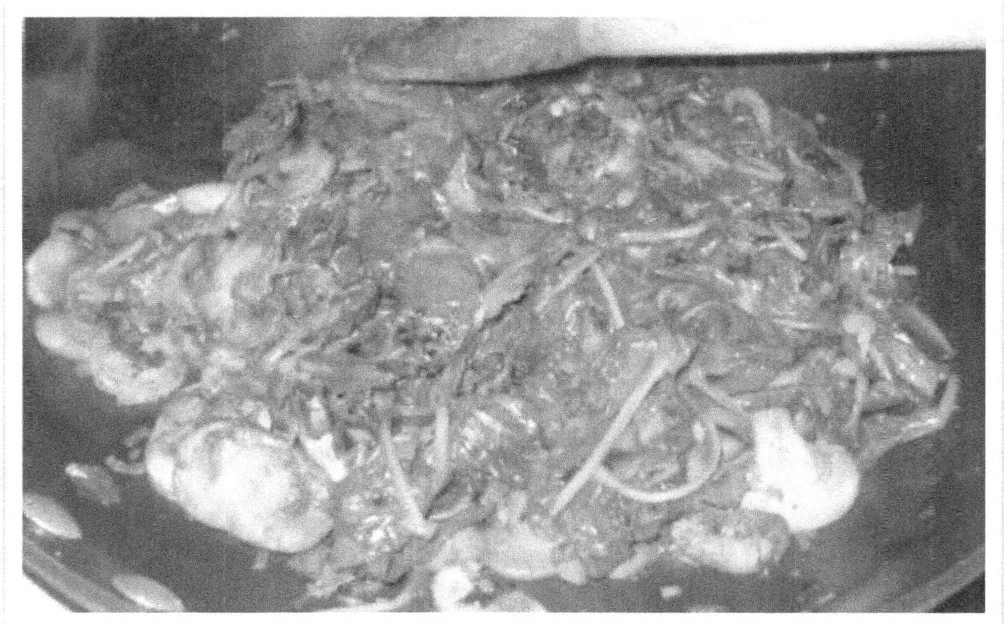

Prep Time: 5 minutes/ Cook Time: 15 minutes / Serves: 4

Ingredients:

- 8 oz mushroom, sliced
- 2 cloves of garlic, minced
- 10 oz spinach
- 2 medium leeks, chopped
- 1/3 tsp dried thyme
- 1/4 tsp black pepper
- 1 Tbsp cooking sherry
- 1 Tbsp nutritional yeast
- 1/3 tsp ground red pepper

Directions:

1. Add 2 tablespoons of water to a large skillet, and place over medium heat. Add the mushrooms, garlic, and leeks. Boil until water evaporates completely. This will take about 4 minutes.
2. Add the spinach, then wait until spinach is wilted enough before you add the thyme, red pepper, and black pepper. Cover, then wait for 2 minutes to add the vinegar and nutritional yeast. Stir.
3. Serve.

Nutritional value per serving:

Calories: 139 kcal, Carbs: 26g Fat: 1.2g, Protein: 11g.

Soups, Stews and Broths

Paleo Chicken Soup

Prep Time: 15 minutes/ Cook Time: 45 minutes / Serves: 4

Ingredients:

- 1 Tbsp coconut oil
- 1-pound ground chicken(organic)
- 2 Tbsp sliced ginger
- 1 cup celery, diced
- 1/2 tsp salt
- 1 cup green onion, sliced with white and green separated
- 3 cups broth
- 1/2 cup carrots, shredded
- 1 tsp ground turmeric
- 1/16 tsp ground turmeric
- 1/4 cup fresh cilantro, packed
- 14 oz full-fat coconut milk
- 1/4 tsp red pepper, crushed

Directions:

1. Pour the coconut oil into a large soup pot, then place over medium heat.
2. When the oil starts to sizzle, add the chicken and ginger. Leave to fry for 5-10 minutes.
3. Pour the garlic in and cook for 2 more minutes.
4. Add 1/2 cup of the white part of the green onions and cook for 1 minute.
5. Add the broth, carrots, cinnamon, and turmeric to the mixture in the pot and increase the heat.
6. Once the broth starts boiling, lower the heat, cover the lid and allow to cook for 20 more minutes. Stir periodically.
7. Add the rest of the green onions (the green part), cilantro, coconut milk and increase the heat once again. Cook until it boils.
8. After boiling, allow to simmer for 10 minutes.
9. Serve as desired.

Nutritional value per serving:

Calories: 480 kcal, Carbs: 20g Fat: 31g, Protein: 36g.

Split Pea Soup

Prep Time: 8 hours 30 minutes/ Cook Time: 2 minutes / Serves: 6

Ingredients:

- 2 quarts cold water
- 2-1/4 cups split peas, dried
- 1-1/2 pounds ham bone
- 2 medium onions, thinly sliced
- 1 medium potato, diced
- 3 medium carrots, chopped
- 3 stalks of celery, chopped
- 1/4 tsp ground black pepper
- 1/3 tsp marjoram, dried

Directions:

1. Soak the peas in cold water overnight. Then drain.
2. Boil the soaked peas with marjoram, ham bone, onion, salt, and pepper. Allow to boil, then simmer for 1-1/2 hours. Stir periodically.
3. Remove the ham bone, slice off the meat, chop and return the meat to the broth
4. Add the potatoes, carrots, and celery. Remove the cover of the pot and continue cooking for about 30-40 minutes.
5. Serve.

Nutritional value per serving:

Calories: 310 kcal, Carbs:57.9g Fat: 1g, Protein: 19.7g.

Black Bean Chili

Prep Time: 20 minutes/ Cook Time: 1hour 15 minutes / Serves: 6

Ingredients:

- 45 oz black beans, undrained
- 14-1/2 oz crushed tomatoes
- 1 Tbsp extra virgin olive oil
- 1 large onion, sliced
- 2 cloves of garlic, minced
- 1-pound ground turkey
- 1-1/2 Tbsp chili powder
- 1 Tbsp dried oregano
- 1 Tbsp dried basil leaves
- 1 Tbsp red wine vinegar

Directions:

1. Pour the olive oil into a large-sized non-stick pot and place over medium heat. Once the oil starts to sizzle, add the onions and garlic, then stir until onions turn translucent.
2. Add the turkey and fry until the meat turns brown.
3. Add the beans, basil, tomatoes, oregano, chili powder, and vinegar. Lower the heat, cover, and allow to simmer for 60.
4. Serve.

Nutritional value per serving:

Calories: 366 kcal, Carbs: 29.6g Fat: 9.2g, Protein: 29.6g.

Pasta Fagioli

Prep Time: 10 minutes/ Cook Time: 1hour 30 minutes / Serves: 6

Ingredients:

- 3 Tbsp extra virgin olive oil
- 1 large onion, sliced
- 2 cloves of garlic, minced
- 15 oz canrellini beans
- 29 oz tomato sauce
- 5-1/2 cups water
- 1 Tbsp dried parsley
- 1 tsp salt
- 1-1/2 tsp cried oregano
- 1-1/2 tsp dried basil leaves
- 1 Tbsp red wine vinegar
- 15 oz navy beans
- 1-pound gluten-free pasta
- 1/3 parmesan cheese, grated

Directions:

1. Pour the olive oil into a large-sized non-stick pot and place over medium heat. Once the oil starts to sizzle, add the onions and garlic, then stir until onions turn translucent.
2. Reduce the heat and stir in the tomato sauce, parsley, basil, cannellini beans, parmesan, navy beans, oregano, salt, and water. Allow to simmer for an hour.
3. Boil the pasta in water for 10 minutes, add a pinch of salt, drain, then stir into soup.
4. Serve.

Nutritional value per serving:

Calories: 403 kcal, Carbs: 68g Fat: 7.6g, Protein: 16.3g.

White Bean Chicken Chili

Prep Time: 10 minutes/ Cook Time: 25 minutes / Serves: 9

Ingredients:

- 2 Tbsp extra virgin olive oil
- 1 large onion, chopped
- 2 cloves of garlic, minced
- 15 oz chicken broth
- 18. 75 oz tomatillos, chopped and drained
- 16 oz tomatoes, diced
- 7 oz green chiles, diced
- 1/2 tsp dried oregano
- 1/2 tsp ground coriander seed
- 1 tsp salt
- 15 oz white beans
- 1/4 ground cumin
- 1-pound cooked chicken, diced
- 2 ears of fresh corn
- 1/3 parmesan cheese, grated

Directions:

1. Pour the olive oil into a large-sized non-stick pot and place over medium heat. Once the oil starts to sizzle, add the onions and garlic, then stir until onions turn translucent.
2. Stir in the tomatoes, broth, chiles, tomatillos, and spices. Allow to boil, then reduce heat, and simmer for 10 minutes.
3. Stir in the corn, beans, and chicken, then simmer for 5 minutes.
4. Season with pepper and salt. Stir.
5. Top with parmesan cheese and serve.

Nutritional value per serving:

Calories: 220 kcal, Carbs: 6.1g Fat: 21.2g, Protein: 20.1g.

Black-eyed Pea Gumbo

Prep Time: 15 minutes/ Cook Time: 55 minutes / Serves: 4

Ingredients:

- 1 Tbsp extra virgin olive oil
- 1 large onion, chopped
- 2 cloves of garlic, minced
- 2 cups chicken broth
- 14 oz tomatoes, diced
- 10 oz tomatoes and green chiles, diced
- 60 oz black-eyed peas
- 1 medium green bell pepper, chopped
- 1 cup of brown rice
- 5 stalks of celery, chopped

Directions:

1. Pour the olive oil into a large-sized non-stick pot and place over medium heat. Once the oil starts to sizzle, add the onions, garlic, celery, and pepper, then stir until celery becomes tender.
2. Stir in the rice, chicken broth, black-eyed peas with juice, diced tomatoes, and diced tomatoes and chiles. Allow to boil, then reduce heat, and simmer for 45 minutes.
3. Serve.

Nutritional value per serving:

Calories: 187 kcal, Carbs: 23.1g Fat: 3.8g, Protein: 15.3g.

Prep Time: 20 minutes/ Cook Time: 4hours 5 minutes / Serves: 4

Ingredients:

- 1 Tbsp extra-virgin olive oil
- 1-1/2 pounds chicken, shredded
- 4 rutabagas, diced and peeled
- 4 medium-sized beets, peeled and diced
- 3 stalks of celery, diced
- 4 medium carrots, diced
- 1 small red onion, diced
- Water, to cover

Directions:

1. Pour the oil into a large soup pot, then place over medium heat.
2. When the oil starts to sizzle, add the chicken. Leave to fry for 3-5 minutes, or until both sides turn brown.
3. Add rutabagas, carrots, beets, red onion, and celery to the pot, then pour enough water to cover the vegetable mixture completely.
4. Reduce the heat and allow to simmer for 4 hours. Keep the vegetable submerged by adding water periodically.
5. Serve.

Nutritional value per serving:

Calories: 111 kcal, Carbs: 12.9g Fat: 2.1g, Protein: 10.7g.

Tomato-Curry Lentil Stew

Prep Time: 10 minutes/ Cook Time: 50 minutes / Serves: 2

Ingredients:

- 1 cup of water
- 1/2 cup dry lentils
- 5 oz stewed tomatoes
- 1 small on on, chopped
- 2 stalks of celery, chopped
- 1/3 tsp curry powder
- 1/2 tsp salt
- 3 cloves of garlic, minced
- 1/2 tsp grcund black pepper

Directions:

1. Mix lentils and water in a medium-sized pot and place on medium heat to bcil.
2. Reduce the heat, stir in the celery, onion, and tomatoes and allow to simmer for 45 minutes. Stir the stew every 15 minutes and add water if necessary. In the last 15 minutes, add the spices; salt, pepper, ga-lic, and curry.
3. After the 45 minutes is complete, remove from heat and serve.

Nutritional value per serving:

Calories: 206 kcal, Carbs: 36.9g Fat: 0.8g, Protein: 13.7g.

Appetizers

Strawberry Pineapple Chicken Bites

Prep Time: 20 minutes/ Cook Time: 20 minutes / Serves: 12

Ingredients:

- 2 Tbsp extra virgin olive oil
- 2 pounds shredded chicken
- 12 oz strawberry preserves
- 8 oz diced pineapples
- 8 oz chili sauce
- 1/2 tsp salt
- 1/2 ground black pepper
- toothpicks

Directions:

1. Pour the olive oil into a skillet and place on medium heat. Add in the shredded chicken, and fry for 5 minutes until all sides have turned brown.
2. Lower the heat and add in the strawberry preserves and chili sauce. Cook for 10 minutes and stir continuously.
3. Add the diced pineapples and season with black pepper and salt. Allow to cook for 2 minutes.
4. Dish into plates and serve with toothpicks.

Nutritional value per serving:

Calories: 187 kcal, Carbs: 23.1g Fat: 3.8g, Protein: 15.3g.

Prep Time: 10 minutes/ Cook Time: 0 minutes / Serves: 6 (12 deviled eggs halves)

Ingredients:

- 6 hard-boiled eggs, halved
- 1 tsp rice wine vinegar
- 1/4 cup mayonnaise
- 1/2 tsp fresh dill, chopped
- 1 tsp Dijon mustard
- 1/4 tsp garlic powder
- 1/8 tsp salt
- 12 fresh dill sprigs

Directions:

1. Carefully remove the egg yolks, and set the egg whites aside.
2. Mash the yolks in a small bowl and mix with the mayonnaise, chopped dill, vinegar, mustard, garlic and salt.
3. Scoop the yolk mixture into the egg whites.
4. Garnish each deviled egg with a sprig of dill.
5. Serve or keep in the refrigerator until ready to eat

Nutritional value per serving:

Calories: 139 kcal, Carbs: 1g Fat: 12.3g, Protein: 6.4g.

Strawberry Bruschetta

Prep Time: 10 minutes/ Cook Time: 5 minutes / Serves: 12

Ingredients:

- 24 slices of gluten-free bread
- 2 cups fresh strawberries, chopped
- 1 Tbsp cream cheese, softened

Directions:

1. Preheat the broiler in the oven to 320°F.
2. Spread the cream cheese on each slice of bread and arrange on a large baking sheet
3. Arrange the bread under the broiler until the bread is lightly toasted. This will take about 1-2 minutes.
4. Bring the bread out from under the broiler and arrange the strawberries on the toast.
5. Place the bread back in the oven for about 5 minutes, then serve.

Nutritional value per serving:

Calories: 120 kcal, Carbs: 23g Fat: 1.6g, Protein: 3.7g.

Spicy Chicken Wings

Prep Time: 15 minutes/ Cook Time: 30 minutes / Serves: 12

Ingredients:

- 12 pieces of chicken wings
- 1-1/2 hot sauce
- 1 cup honey
- 3/4 cup cream cheese
- 1/3 garlic salt
- 1/3 tsp ground black pepper
- 1 tsp cayenne powder

Directions:

1. Preheat the outdoor grill
2. Lightly oil the grate of the grill, then arrange the chicken on the grill. While periodically turning the chicken, grill for 8-12 minutes.
3. Mix the cream cheese, hot sauce, cayenne pepper, garlic salt, honey, and black pepper in a saucepan, then place on medium heat. Simmer for 10 minutes, then coat the sauce on the grilled chicken wings.

Nutritional value per serving:

Calories: 356 kcal, Carbs: 23.9g Fat: 22.7g, Protein: 15.6g.

Shrimp Scamp

Prep Time: 15 minutes/ Cook Time: 6 minutes / Serves: 4

Ingredients:

- 2 pounds large shrimp, deveined and peeled
- 6 Tbsp unsalted cream cheese, melted
- 1/4 cup extra virgin olive oil
- 1 Tbsp minced garlic
- 1 Tbsp minced shallots
- 2 Tbsp fresh chives, minced
- Salt, to taste
- 1/2 tsp ground pepper
- 1/2 tsp paprika

Directions:

1. Preheat the grill to high temperature
2. Mix the cream cheese, garlic, olive oil, chives, shallots, pepper, salt, paprika in a large bowl.
3. Add in the shrimp to the mixture and toss to coat it.
4. Lightly oil the grate of the grill.
5. Grill the shrimp, making sure both sides are done before removing them.
6. Serve.

Nutritional value per serving:

Calories: 302 kcal, Carbs: 0.9g Fat: 21.8g, Protein: 25g.

Salads and Smoothies

Mediterranean Greek Cucumber Salad

Prep Time: 15 minutes/ Cook Time: 0 minutes / Serves: 4

Ingredients:

- 2 medium-size cucumbers, diced
- 1 cup grape tomatoes
- 1/4 cup sliced red onion
- 1/2 tsp sea salt
- 1/4 tsp black pepper
- 1 tsp fresh basil, chopped
- 1 tsp fresh parsley, chopped
- 1 tsp fresh oregano, chopped
- 1 tsp minced garlic
- 1 tsp red wine vinegar
- 2 tsp extra virgin olive oil
- 1/8 tsp red pepper, crushed
- 1/2 cup crumbled feta cheese

Directions:

5. Pour the cucumber, red onions, and tomatoes into a medium-sized bowl and add salt and pepper. Mix the ingredients and allow to rest for 10 minutes to ensure the maximum blend of the juices from the cucumber and tomatoes.
6. After resting, add the basil, oregano, parsley, garlic, vinegar, red pepper, and olive oil. Stir until well combined.
7. Allow to marinate for 5 minutes, then stir. Serve as desired.

Nutritional value per serving:

Calories: 80kcal, Carbs: 13g Fat: 0g, Protein: 4g.

Carrot and Apple Slaw

Prep Time: 5 minutes/ Cook Time: 0 minutes / Serves: 6

Ingredients:

- 10 oz shredded carrots
- 4 cups green apples, cut into matchsticks
- 5 cups shredded purple cabbage
- 1/4 cup mayonnaise
- 1 cup raisins
- 3 Tbsp nonfat Greek yogurt
- 3 Tbsp rice vinegar
- 1/2 tsp celery seeds
- 1/2 tsp salt
- 3 Tbsp honey

Directions:

1. In a medium bowl, mix the yogurt, mayonnaise, vinegar, honey, celery, and salt.
2. Add in the carrots, raisins, and apples.
3. Serve with dressing or refrigerate until ready to serve

Nutritional value per serving:

Calories: 236 kcal, Carbs: 43g Fat: 5g, Protein: 10g.

Blueberry Smoothie

Prep Time: 3 minutes/ Cook Time:0 minutes / Serves: 2

Ingredients:

- 1 cup blueberries
- 1/2 cup Greek yogurt
- 1/4 tsp vanilla extract
- 1/2 cup freshly squeezed orange
- 1/2 tsp cinnamon
- 3 ice cubes

Directions:

1. Pour all the ingredients (except ice) into a blender and blend for 60 seconds
2. Add the ice and blend until smooth. This may take another 60 seconds.

Nutritional value per serving:

Calories: 195kcal. Carbs: 13.9g Fat: 10.6g, Protein: 7.5g.

Guacamole Salad

Prep Time: 5 minutes/ Cook Time: 0 minutes / Serves: 4

Ingredients:

- 2 avocados, diced
- 2 garden cucumbers, chopped
- 2 cups of tomatoes, sliced
- 1 small red/brown onion
- 2 scallions, sliced
- 1 red pepper, chopped and deseeded
- 1/2 cup pickled jalapenos
- 1 bunch chopped coriander
- 2 Tbsp lime juice
- 4 Tbsp extra virgin olive oil
- 1 Tbsp apple cider vinegar
- Salt, to taste

Directions:

1. Wash the vegetable ingredients and mix the cucumber, avocados, tomatoes, onion, scallion, jalapenos, coriander, and red pepper in a medium-sized bowl.
2. Prepare the dressing in a separate bowl by mixing the lime juice, apple cider vinegar, and olive oil. Add salt and pepper as desired.
3. Serve the salad into plates and drizzle the dressing over it.

Nutritional value per serving:

Calories: 104kcal, Carbs: 13g Fat: 5.5g, Protein: 1.2g.

Red Quinoa Salad

Prep Time: 5 minutes/ Cook Time: 15 minutes / Serves: 2

Ingredients:

- 1/2 cup red quinoa, dry
- 1 cup of water
- 1/4 cup red onion, diced
- 1/2 cup black beans, rinsed and drained
- 1/2 Tbsp extra-virgin olive oil
- 1 Tbsp balsamic vinegar

Directions:

1. Pour the quinoa into a bowl and rinse under cold water.
2. Transfer the quinoa into a medium-sized saucepot, add water, and place over medium heat to boil for 15 minutes.
3. Once the quinoa is ready, add the rest of the *Ingredients:* red onion, black beans, extra virgin olive oil, and balsamic vinegar. Stir until well combined.
4. Serve.

Nutritional value per serving:

Calories: 280kcal, Carbs: 32g Fat: 10g, Protein: 16g.

Drinks

Green Dream Hemp Seed Smoothie

Prep Time: 5 minutes/ Cook Time: 0 minutes / Serves: 4

Ingredients:

- 2 cups frozen pineapple
- 2 cups frozen mango
- 2 cups spinach, packed
- 2 cups hemp seed milk, homemade
- 1/4 tsp coconut extract
- 3 tsp hemp seed, hulled

Directions:

1. Put the frozen mango, spinach, pineapple, coconut extract, hemp seed, and hemp seed milk into a high-speed blender.
2. Blend until completely smooth.
3. Serve as desired.

Nutritional value per serving:

Calories: 260 kcal, Carbs: 28g Fat: 12g, Protein: 11g.

Non-dairy Coconut Milk Yogurt (Homemade)

Prep Time: 10 minutes/ Cook Time: 24-48 hours / Serves: 4

Ingredients:

- 14 oz full-fat coconut milk
- 1/8 tsp sea salt
- 1/2 tsp maple syrup, pure
- 2 probiot c capsules
- 2 scoops unflavored collagen peptides

Directions:

1. Sterilize the glass jar that will hold the yogurt by submerging in boiling water.
2. Add the coconut milk to the sterile glass jar and stir.
3. Sprinkle the contents of the probiotic capsules into the coconut milk and st r vigorously.
4. Close the lid of the jar and allow the mixture to ferment for 24- 48hours. Shake occasionally to aid the fermentation process.
5. After 24-48 hours, refrigerate the mixture. This is done to thicken the mixture.
6. Stir in the collagen peptides, maple syrup, and sea salt when ready to serve.
7. The mixture must be stored in a refrigerator and consumed within 7 days.

Nutritional value per serving:

Calories: 244 kcal, Carbs: 18.2g Fat: 23g, Protein: 14g.

Prep Time: 10 minutes/ Cook Time: 10 minutes / Serves: 2

Ingredients:

- 1 cup packed baby spinach
- 2 frozen bananas
- 1/2 avocado, scooped and pitted
- 1/4 cup mint leaves, fresh
- 1 tsp vanilla extract, pure
- 1 cup homemade hemp seed milk.
- Plant-based whipped cream, optional and as desired
- Vegan chocolate chips, optional and as desired

Directions:

1. Blend the bananas, avocado, spinach, mint leaves, hemp seed milk, and vanilla extract together until smooth and creamy. This may take about 60-90 seconds.
2. The drink is ready to be served. You can top with whipped cream and chocolate chips as desired

Nutritional value per serving:

Calories: 200 kcal, Carbs: 33g Fat: 10g, Protein: 3g.

Summer Squash Smoothie Infused with CBD

Prep Time: 5 minutes/ Cook Time: 5 minutes / Serves: 2

Ingredients:

- 6 oz yellow squash, diced and seeded
- 4 oz frozen preaches
- 1/2 large banana
- 2 scoops unflavored collagen protein powder
- 1 cup ice
- 1 Tbsp lemon juice
- 1 Tbsp honey
- 1 tsp ground turmeric
- 1/16 tsp ground cinnamon
- 1ml CBD oil
- 1/16 tsp ground black pepper
- 1 large mint leaf, optional

Directions:

1. Blend all the ingredients in a high-speed blender for about 60-90 seconds.
2. Serve into cups and enjoy.

Nutritional value per serving:

Calories: 250 kcal, Carbs: 41g Fat: 7g, Protein: 9g.

Watermelon Shooter Shots Infused with CBD

Prep Time: 5 minutes/ Cook Time: 5 minutes / Serves: 4

Ingredients:

- 5 oz watermelon puree
- 2-1/2 oz apple cider vinegar
- 1 Tbsp honey
- 1 ml CBD oil
- 1/16 tsp pumpkin pie spice

Directions:

1. Puree the watermelon first if not done already and measure out 5 oz.
2. Add the honey, apple cider vinegar, and pumpkin pie spice to the puree and blend until smooth (usually 60-90 seconds).
3. Add the CBD and stir gently.
4. The drink is ready to be served.

Nutritional value per serving:

Calories: 30 kcal, Carbs: 7g Fat: 0g, Protein: 0g.

Side Dishes and Desserts

Green Juice Popsicles

Prep Time: 6 hours+ / Cook Time: 0 minutes / Serves: 6-8

Ingredients:

- 2 large apples, green
- 2 cups spinach, chopped
- 1 cup pineapple, diced
- 1 lime, sliced and deseeded
- 1 large green cucumber

Directions:

1. Juice the pineapple, apple, spinach, cucumber, and lime by blending.
2. Once smooth, pour the juice into popsicle molds or ice cube trays until they are ¾ full.
3. Freeze for 30 minutes then insert the popsicle sticks
4. Freeze overnight, or for about 6 hours until the popsicle is frozen solid.

Nutritional value per serving:

Calories: 42 kcal, Carbs: 11g Fat: 0g, Protein: 1g

Brazil Nut Brownies

Prep Time: 30 minutes/ Cook Time: 30 minutes / Serves: 9

Ingredients:

- Nonstick cooking spray
- 1/3 cup honey
- 2 large eggs
- 1 tsp salt
- 1/2 cup sweet cherries, dried
- 1/3 cup Brazil nuts, chopped
- 1/4 cup coconut oil

- 2 tsp granulated sugar
- 1 tsp vanilla extract
- 1/2 gluten-free baking flour
- 1/2 cup 2% plain yogurt
- 1/3 cup dark chocolate cocoa powder, unsweetened
- 1/2 tsp baking powder

Directions:

1. Preheat the oven to 375°F, place the rack in the middle of the oven and coat the baking pan with nonstick spray.
2. In a large bowl, mix the sugar, oil, and honey. Beat until well blended. Add in the eggs and vanilla extract and keep beating. When well combined, add the yogurt and beat until the batter becomes smooth.
3. In another large bowl, mix the flour, baking powder, cocoa powder, and salt.
4. While beating continuously, add the flour mixture to the egg mixture and keep beating until the batter is well combined.
5. Add in the Brazil nuts and stir.
6. Pour the batter on the prepared baking pan. Arrange the cherries on the batter, taking into consideration how the cherries will be positioned when the brownie is divided into squares.
7. Bake until the brownies are set. This may take up to 20 minutes. When ready, remove the baking pan from the oven and allow to cool for 5 minutes.
8. Cut the brownies into square pieces and serve.

Nutritional value per serving:

Calories: 240 kcal, Carbs: 33g Fat: 25g, Protein: 4g.

Banana Sushi

Prep Time: 10 minutes/ Cook Time: 0 minutes / Serves: 2

Ingredients:

- 1 large banana
- 1 Tbsp hemp seed cream cheese
- 1 Tbsp hemp seeds
- 1/2 cup granola
- 1 tsp chocolate chips

Directions:

1. Get a plastic bag, add the granola, chocolate chips, hemp seeds, then push all the air out and seal tight.
2. With a rolling pin, crush all the cereal within the plastic bag into pieces.
3. Peel the banana and coat completely with hemp seed cream cheese.
4. Open the plastic bag and pour the contents on a chopping board.
5. Roll the coated banana over the cereals on the chopping board and gently press to ensure the cereals stick without squishing the banana.
6. Divide the banana into two equal pieces and serve.

Nutritional value per serving:

Calories: 67.5 kcal, Carbs: 10.2g Fat: 2.3g, Protein: 1.9g.

Mango Fruit Tart

Prep Time: 20 minutes/ Cook Time: 15 minutes / Serves: 10 serves

Ingredients:

Tart Crust
- 15 Medjool dates, pitted and dried.
- 3/4 cup cashews, raw and unsalted
- 2 Tbsp unsweetened coconut flakes, shredded
- 1 Tbsp melted coconut oil

Mango cream
- 3/4 cup coconut milk yogurt, homemade
- 3/4 cup fresh mango, sliced

Toppings
- 1 cup mango, diced
- 1/2 cup raspberries
- 1/2 cup blackberries
- 1/2 cup blueberries

Mango glaze
- 1 Tbsp mango preserves
- 1 tsp water

Directions:

1. Preheat the oven to 350°F
2. Blend the Medjool dates, coconut flakes, cashew nuts, and coconut oil in a food processor until a fine consistency is obtained.
3. Coat the date blend on the outside and bottom side of a tart tin pan, then bake for about 15 minutes. Remove from oven and allow to cool before removing the crust from the tart tin.
4. Blend the yogurt and mango in either a food processor or blender. Once smooth, pour it into date crust and refrigerate until it set. This may take about 20 minutes
5. For toppings, add the diced mango, raspberries, blackberries, and blackberries.
6. Mix the mango preserves and water in a small bowl, microwave for 25 seconds and stir to make the glaze.
7. Brush the glaze over the mango tart and serve.

Nutritional value per serving:

Calories: 18 kcal, Carbs: -g Fat: -g, Protein: -g.

Coconut Rice Pudding

Prep Time: 5 minutes/ Cook Time: 25 minutes / Serves: 8

Ingredients:

- 2 cups jasmine rice
- 4-1/2 unsweetened coconut milk
- 2 Tbsp coconut cream
- 2 tsp ground cinnamon
- 2 Tbsp maple syrup
- 1/2 tsp ground turmeric
- 1-1/2 tsp vanilla extract
- 1/2 tsp ground ginger
- 1/2 cup golden raisins
- 1/2 tsp coconut extract

Directions:

1. Pour 3-1/2 cups of coconut milk beverage into an Instant pot and add the jasmine rice. Cover the lid tightly and cook at high pressure for 3 minutes. After which, use natural release pressure for ten minutes, then use quick pressure release to remove any pressure leftover
2. Stir in the maple syrup, coconut cream, turmeric, ground cinnamon, golden raisins, coconut and vanilla extract.
3. The leftover coconut milk beverage should be used at your discretion, it depends on whether you like your pudding thick or runny.
4. Serve as desired.

Nutritional value per serving:

Calories: 30 kcal, Carbs: 7g Fat: 0g, Protein: 0g.

Fruit Spring Rolls

Prep Time: 15 minutes/ Cook Time: 0 minutes / Serves: 20

Ingredients:

Spring Rolls
- 1 cup sliced strawberries
- 1 cup blueberries
- 1 cup of watermelon, sliced diagonally into matchsticks
- 1 small zucchini, spiralized
- 2 lemons, zested
- 1 can no-salt-added beets, juice drained and reserved

- 1/4 cup mint, freshly chopped
- 20 rice paper rolls

Mint Dip
- 1/2 cup strawberries, sliced
- 1 Tbsp mint leaves
- 1/2 cup coconut milk-yogurt
- 1/2 tsp lemon juice

Directions:

1. In a small bowl, mix 1/2 cup of water and 1/2 cup beet juice.
2. Moisten your work surface (cutting board) to prevent the rice paper from sticking to the surface.
3. Dip the rice paper roll into the water and beet juice mixture for 20 seconds. It will become pliable but still be firm.
4. Lay the paper roll on the wet cutting board, then add the ingredients quickly. Start with the strawberries, then watermelon, citrus vest, watermelon, mint, finish with the zucchini.
5. Roll quickly to ensure your wrapper doesn't lose moisture or become mushy, and ensure the wrapper isn't overfilled. To roll the wrapper, start by stretching the left side of the wrapper over the ingredients, tuck it in, roll for a bit then tuck in the top and bottom flaps and then keep rolling until you reach the edge of the other side.
6. Repeat the steps 3-5 for as many rolls as possible.
7. For the mint dip, blend the yogurt, mint, strawberries, and lemon juice in a food processor for 90 seconds. Pair with spring rolls and enjoy.

Nutritional value per serving:

Calories: 131 kcal, Carbs: 18g Fat: 3g, Protein: 9g.

Deep-fried Zucchini

Prep Time: 5 minutes/ Cook Time: 15 minutes / Serves: 6

Ingredients:

- 4 medium zucchinis, trimmed and sliced
- 3 cups Sunflower oil
- 1/4 cup cornstarch
- 3/4 cup all-purpose flour
- 1/4 tsp. pepper
- 1 tsp. salt, divided

Directions:

1. Add the sunflower oil to a deep skillet until it is about 3 inches deep, then place over medium heat.
2. Mix the flour, 1/2 teaspoon salt, cornstarch, and pepper in a bowl, then dredge the Zucchini in the flour and shake off the excess.
3. When the oil reaches about 370^{0}F, add the flour-coated zucchini to the oil and fry for 2 minutes, then arrange on a tray with paper towels to absorb excess oil.
4. Season with salt to taste and serve immediately.

Nutritional value per serving:

Calories: 320kcal, Carbs: 12g Fat: 29g, Protein: 8g

Conclusion

There you have it, 70 remarkable dishes to help you get started. *Thyroid Healing Diet Cookbook* has fulfilled its promises to educate you on the effects of food on the thyroid, the types of food to eat, and what to avoid. Now, it's up to you to eat for your health.

This change in lifestyle will come with a lot of difficulties and temptations. However, as you must know by now, nothing great comes easy, and nothing easy can ever equate to greatness. With confidence and endurance, you are sure to overcome all those temptations.

Keep eating right and stay healthy!

Appendix I: Standard U.S Metric Measurement Conversion Table

VOLUME CONVERSIONS

U.S. Volume Measure	Metric Equivalent
1/8 tsp. (tsp)	0.5 milliliter
1/4 teaspoon	1 milliliter
1/2 teaspoon	2 milliliters
1 teaspoon	5 milliliters
1/2 tablespoon (Tbsp)	7 milliliters
1 tablespoon (3 tsp)	15 milliliters
2 tablespoons	30 milliliters
1/4 cup	60 milliliters
1/3 cup	90 milliliters
1/2 cup	125 milliliters
2/3 cup	160 milliliters
3/4 cup	180 milliliters
1 cup	250 milliliters

WEIGHT CONVERSIONS

U.S Weight Measure	Metric Equivalent
1/2 ounce (oz)	15 grams
1 ounce	30 grams
2 ounces	60 grams
3 ounces	85 grams
1/4 pound (4 ounces)	115 grams
1/2 pound (8 ounces)	225 grams
3/4 pound (12 ounces)	340 grams
1 pound (16 ounces)	454 grams

OVEN TEMPERATURE CONVERSIONS

Degrees Fahrenheit	Degrees Celsius
350°F	180°C
375°F	190°C
400°F	205°C
425°F	220°C

Appendix II: Related Websites or Books

Emily Kyle, 2018. The 30-Minute Thyroid Cookbook: 125 Healing Recipes for Hypothyroidism and Hashimoto's 1st Edition. *Rockridge Press.*

Joel Fuhrman, 2013. Eat to Live Cookbook: 200 Delicious Nutrient-Rich Recipes for Fast and Sustained Weight Loss, Reversing Disease, and Lifelong Health. *Harper Collins Publisher.*

Dick Logue, 2012. 1001 Heart Healthy Recipes. *Fair Winds Press*

www.rebootwithjoe.com

www.allrecipes.com

www.thyroidrelish.com

www.emilykylenutrition.com

https://www.uofmhealth.org/conditions-treatments/endocrinology-diabetes-and-metabolism/hyperthyroidism-and-graves-disease

https://my.clevelandclinic.org/health/diseases/8541-thyroid-disease

https://www.google.com/amp/s/www.endocrineweb.com/amp/13683

https://www.livescience.com/58771-thyroid-gland-facts.html

https://www.webmd.com/women/picture-of-the-thyroid

https://www.medicinenet.com/thyroid_disorders/article.htm#what_are_thyroid_disorders

https://www.ncbi.nlm.nih.gov/books/NBK279388/